twelve principles

For Anastasia, Liam, Zoë and Tarn,

children of the twenty-first century

twelve principles

Living with integrity in the twenty-first century

Martin Hawes

FINCH PUBLISHING
SYDNEY

twelve

1. One people
Humanity is one people. There is no 'them'; there's only us.

2. One planet
The Earth is our home. When we disrespect it, we endanger all life including our own.

3. Responsibility
Each of us bears a share of responsibility for our communities, and hence for the world as a whole.

4. Making a difference
Each of us can contribute to making the world a safer, happier place to live.

5. Learning
Living requires constant learning, and questioning can help free our minds to learn.

6. Seeing
Being aware means seeing with our hearts as well as our minds.

principles

7. Self-awareness

Self-awareness helps free us from the fear and ignorance that obstruct relationship.

8. Global awareness

To live responsibly we need to understand the global consequences of our actions.

9. Respect

To respect is to acknowledge the sacred in the Earth and in all living things.

10. Simplicity

When we are inwardly rich, outwardly we need very little.

11. Love

When we feel a sense of communion with the universe, we can act from love.

12. Integrity

Integrity is the clarity of intention that comes with understanding and love.

Foreword

Many people are concerned about the state of the world but are unsure where the solution lies or how they can contribute to finding it. *Twelve Principles* is a timely reminder that the global crisis is at root a crisis in values, and that, by our thoughts and actions, each of us has an impact on what is happening in the world around us. In compelling language, Martin Hawes challenges the prevailing ethic of materialism and offers guidelines for a peaceful and sustainable future. His underlying message is that by living with integrity we can transform this age of crisis and pessimism into one of opportunity and optimism.

Martin has been a philosophical friend of mine since the Franklin River Blockade twenty years ago. He thinks and writes with a clarity that comes from decades of wilderness journeys and philosophical inquiry. The magnificent photos, some of them taken by Martin himself, bear witness to what is at stake on this planet and illustrate his claim that 'being aware means seeing with our hearts as well as our minds'.

Twelve Principles includes personal accounts by twelve extraordinary people who are exploring creative ways to meet the challenges of the modern world. Their stories show that the alternatives Martin Hawes proposes are practical and achievable — and remind us that we can each contribute in our own special way to ensuring the world's future.

Bob Brown
Senator, Australian Greens

Contents

Principles of Action

Introduction

The twenty-first century will be a time of unprecedented challenge and change. Within the next few decades the combined effects of global warming, environmental decline and shortages of vital resources could cause catastrophic disruptions, affecting the lives of billions of people. More than two billion people are already destitute, and humanity is living under the ever-present threat – and with the frequent reality – of terrorism and war.

Faced with this extraordinary crisis, it is natural to ask, 'What can I do?'. Can individuals make a difference or are world events beyond our control?

Each of us *can* make a difference. We need to act with integrity and with an awareness of how our actions affect the world in which we live. The principles in this book explore aspects of our relationship with the world around us, and suggest ways in which we can change that relationship.

These principles are windows into alternative ways of thinking and living. Don't follow them – because if you try to live by a code you will cease to use your own intelligence. Examine them with a critical mind and decide for yourself what is true or false. Once you perceive the truth of something, that perception brings understanding, and you will not need to follow an idea.

The list of principles in this book is not definitive. It doesn't include nonviolence, for example – although non-violence is implicit in these twelve principles. In a sense, all the principles are facets of a single proposition:

namely, that to live intelligently we need to be aware that we are connected to the whole of life.

Writing this book has been both a great privilege and a revelation. I feel greatly privileged to have interviewed the inspiring people who tell their stories here. The revelation was the discovery of hundreds of similar stories — stories most of us never hear. I was discovering, in the midst of this world of crisis and strife, a parallel world of courage and hope. The more people of courage that I encounter, the more I become convinced that each of us has the opportunity to write our own stories of hope.

Martin Hawes
Cygnet, Tasmania

Principles

of

Relationship

I. One people

Humanity is

one people.

There is no 'them';

there's only us.

Humanity is one people. We all belong to a single tribe. There is no 'our people' and 'their people'; there is only humanity. There is no 'them'; there's only us.

Some of us are dark-skinned and some of us are pale. Some of us live in penthouses and others live in packing crates. But we all come naked into the world and we will enrich the same Earth when we die. A smile is a smile and tears are tears whatever the colour of the face.

Your beliefs may be different from mine. But you and I both have beliefs. We all have fears, hopes, dreams, loves, sorrows and aspirations. We are all, in various ways, searching for meaning in our lives.

The world is fragmented along ethnic, religious, economic and political lines. There is conflict between North and South, Muslims and Christians, employers and workers, white and black. We live in separate countries and clans with conflicting interests and ideals. But we don't have to live this way.

In the late 1990s I spent a year at a school where a hundred students and adults from all over the world live, work and study together. At the reception desk one can overhear conversations in French, Ukrainian, Spanish, Japanese or any of a dozen other languages. (English is the school's lingua franca.) Within the grounds of the school no single country is represented by more than a handful of students or teachers, so nationalism has no meaning. Yet the school has a wonderful sense of community.

The urge to belong is deeply ingrained in human consciousness. Our distant ancestors lived in tribes, and in our own way we are also tribal. Most of us want to feel that we are part of a community, whether that community is a nation, an ethnic group or a local football club. Many of us feel a sense of connection to the land we live on. It is good to feel that we belong — but not if this leads to disputes over land and divisions between communities. Can we feel a sense of belonging without creating division? Can we belong to all humanity, and indeed to all of life?

Belonging helps us to feel secure. But when we identify ourselves with an exclusive 'us' we automatically create a 'them', and this division creates conflict that undermines our security. I may feel comparatively safe calling myself an American, a Russian, an Israeli or an Indian; but the pursuit by separate nations of their so-called national interests creates global instability and ultimately leads to war.

Many of us are conditioned from childhood to believe that 'we' are separate from 'them'. And beliefs like this tend to be self-fulfilling. If I believe you are my enemy I will treat you as such – inciting you to *become* my enemy. By the time we are shooting at each other it will be hard to see that we are fighting over an illusion. On Christmas Day in 1914, British and German soldiers emerged from the muddy horror of the Western Front and played football together between the trenches. When they put down their weapons, they realised they were all ordinary men.

What about dictators, terrorists and others who threaten human security? Aren't we justified in calling such people our enemies? If we are, then let us also blacklist people and nations that consume more than their fair share of the world's resources, or that threaten humanity's ecological security with excessive greenhouse gas emissions. By all means let's isolate 'rogue states' – when our own governments stop waging war for oil and threatening world security with weapons of mass destruction.

Working for a common cause can bring a sense of solidarity, especially to people who are struggling against oppression. These people have the right to resist oppression and to defend their cultural identities. But the love of freedom cuts across cultural and ethnic boundaries. In May 2000 a quarter of a million non-Aboriginal Australians marched in Sydney alongside Aborigines in support of the Aboriginal struggle for justice and self-determination.

The idea that 'we' are separate from 'them' allows the rich to turn a blind eye to the privations of the poor. By the beginning of the twenty-first century, people in the wealthiest 20 percent of the world's population were 80 times richer than their counterparts in the poorest 20 percent. While rich nations send spacecraft to find water on Mars, more than a billion people on Earth lack access to water that's safe to drink.

Divided, we lack the resolve to address the global problems that confront us. Until now, efforts to restrict greenhouse gas emissions have been undermined by a handful of corporations and wealthy nations that see such restrictions as a threat to their economic interests. But none of these corporations or nations will benefit if sea levels rise by several metres, inundating coastal cities and destroying economies.

The problems that confront humanity demand a global response. They demand that we put our labels aside and cooperate as one community. Can we do this? We can, if we acknowledge that the old divisions are no longer valid and that every person on Earth has the right to economic security and political freedom.

An organisation called Seeds of Peace arranges annual summer camps for young people from the Middle East, the Balkans, South Asia and other regions where there are long-standing divisions between nations and ethnic groups. Some of the young people who attend these camps make lifelong friends with people they had formerly regarded as enemies. Speaking of the Pakistani students she had met, one fourteen-year-old Indian participant said, 'They're just like us, exactly like us. If we are so similar we have nothing to fight about.'

Greenpeace, Amnesty International and Global Greens are examples of international organisations whose memberships and policies cut across traditional ethnic and national boundaries. The United Nations Declaration on the Rights of the Child, and the recent establishment of the International Court of Justice in The Hague, are steps towards universal opportunity and justice. The campaign to cancel Third World debt demonstrates that many people in the developed world want to see a better deal for the South.

As communities, we can foster global cooperation by promoting the kinds of crosscultural exchanges that Seeds of Peace and similar organisations have initiated. We can do that by, for example, encouraging local schools to initiate crosscultural programs. The village of Hawkshead (pop. 600) in northern England recently established links with the village of Capari (pop. 500) in southern Macedonia, to promote understanding between two vastly different European cultures.

As individuals, we need to question our beliefs and to examine the ways in which our lifestyles and political choices impact on the rest of the world. We need to question our acceptance of violence and insist that our governments invest as lavishly in peace and international cooperation as they have traditionally invested in preparing for war.

The walls that divide us will remain only for as long as they remain in our minds. The moment we see that our divisions are false we can start to build a world without frontiers. Then we will see that when we kill our so-called enemies we are killing our own people. Then we will see that the poor and disadvantaged are 'us'.

In Afghanistan, a quarter of all children die before the age of five. These are our people.

In Zambia, Aids is killing almost as many teachers as the country can train each year. These are our people.

In China, factory workers are labouring up to sixteen hours a day for as little as twelve cents per hour. In Chile, the relatives of people killed or 'disappeared' by the Pinochet regime are still struggling for justice.

Our people.

Songs of healing

Ibrahim Alex Bangura

SIERRA LEONE

My earliest memories of Sierra Leone are of a peaceful and beautiful country. Then the fighting and killing started. In the early 1990s the war was confined to the south, but by the time I was fourteen it had spread to the city and had stopped me from going to school altogether. For most of my childhood, guns and bombs were the order of the day.

The war affected my country in so many ways. It devastated the economy to such an extent that by the year 2000 Sierra Leone was at the very bottom of the United Nations human-development list. It caused a decline in education and a decay of the political system. Tens of thousands of people were killed and more than 2 million people – 40 percent of the population – were displaced. As in most recent wars, women and children suffered the most.

I first heard about PeaceLinks when members of the organisation came to visit my primary school. They came with the message that we could put the trauma of the past behind us and contribute meaningfully to society. I was interested in what they were saying but what attracted me most were their songs – they sang very beautiful songs. As it happened, one of my teachers knew the founder of PeaceLinks, and he encouraged me to get involved.

I was ten years old when I started helping with the PeaceLinks Outreach Program. The program coordinators would give me a short speech to memorise and I'd go out in front of a group of other children and get maybe a third of it right! I also started performing music, and the more I rehearsed the more I came to appreciate how powerful and meaningful music can be. Eventually a group of us formed a band called Peacelinks Musical Youths, and for several years now we've been writing and performing songs about our experiences of the war and our hopes for the future. We're currently recording our third album and we performed our song 'Time to Abolish War' at the Appeal for Peace Conference in The Hague in 1999.

PeaceLinks is currently focusing on rehabilitating former child combatants. Most of these kids are deeply traumatised and many of them have lost one or both of their parents. Imagine what it must be like to be an orphan, especially in a country like this. We have some children here whose

parents were murdered right in front of them. That is trauma for life. PeaceLinks is trying to de-traumatise them and help them return to civil society.

We make no distinction between former child soldiers and victims. Most of the children who took up arms had no choice; they would have been butchered if they had refused. Many of them are ashamed, and reluctant to talk about what they did in the war. They don't even like us referring to them as ex-child combatants, so we call them war-affected children.

One of the basic rules of our program is that what happened in the jungle is past and forgotten. Some of the children who come to us were fighting in opposing camps, so there can be tension between them here. We tell them that here we see ourselves as brothers, as the same people. We are trying to build a unified nation, a nation that will never again accept war. So we encourage the children to walk together, play together and dance together. When we see them doing that we know they have been able to overcome the past.

The war has had a major impact on the education of these children, so we give them some informal schooling, including basic maths and English. We help them to write their names and understand simple English phrases like 'Good morning' and 'Hello, how are you?' We teach them some minor spelling and how to write simple letters. With the help of other agencies like Amnesty International, we are putting these children in touch with kids their own age in other parts of the world so that they can share their stories and develop ongoing friendships.

We are also trying to give these children basic skills so they can fend for themselves when they leave our program. We've just started weaving and soap-making classes, and we are teaching tie-dyeing to some of the girls. We teach the children about their basic rights and some aspects of the Convention on the Rights of the Child. We are also teaching them art and music in the hope that some of them will be able to make a living as professional artists. I'm not qualified to teach music – I learnt guitar and keyboards mainly by ear – but when they hear our band and see that we are the same age as them, they realise what is possible. It's difficult to make a living as an artist in Sierra Leone, but you can succeed if you find a way to sell your work abroad.

'My experiences of this war have convinced me that change cannot be achieved through violence.'

PeaceLinks continues to visit schools and community groups, including communities that are not reached by other NGOs. In 2001 our program reached more than 5000 children and 3000 disadvantaged adults. I recently went with our director to Makeni, a town in central Sierra Leone that was under rebel siege for three years. There are many war-affected children in the area, and people there are keen for us to establish our programs. We don't have the funding for this yet but we are hoping to get it soon. Every year on the International Day of Peace, PeaceLinks organises a large gathering where we hold seminars and ceremonies. We use this opportunity to distribute educational materials and secondhand clothing to needy children. We also have regular radio programs on issues such as child development, youth unemployment and the experiences of child soldiers. We encourage youths to talk on these programs and some of them have used the opportunity to make a public apology for what they did in the war.

My visit to the Netherlands in 1999 had an enormous impact on my life. Like every Sierra Leonean I used to dream of visiting the West, but I never imagined that I would see myself in one of those wonderful cities or have the opportunity to represent my country at an international forum. I felt highly honoured; words are inadequate to express my appreciation. Since that time, people from all over the world have contacted me, and being well known has made it easier for me to continue my work.

My experiences of this war have convinced me that change cannot be achieved through violence. When the rebels attacked our country many people argued that we needed to use the army to defeat them, but in the end peace was achieved only through dialogue and negotiation. If you want to effect change you don't have to use violence; you can go to the ballot box, you can use the media, you can demonstrate in the streets. In Africa, especially, the media function as an opposing voice to the government's. At The Hague I realised the importance of peace education as a way of ensuring that war becomes a thing of the past.

I have just completed my secondary school exams and I'm looking forward to going to university. I hope to get a degree so that I can work with different organisations, including the United Nations. I'd like to have the opportunity to stand up at different international forums and advocate for my country and for underprivileged children everywhere.

The young people in Sierra Leone face enormous difficulties. They are battling with poverty, illiteracy, unemployment and a lack of housing. Many of them have had no schooling, and there is no social security to fall back on. Tens of thousands of young people are in this situation; if it weren't for humanitarian agencies, they would not survive. The security situation here is also uncertain: the last war spread to Sierra Leone from Liberia and the same situation threatens us again. If these problems aren't addressed there's a risk that we will go back to square one.

The West must accept some responsibility for what is happening in places like Sierra Leone. The gap between rich and poor nations is vast, and under globalisation it is increasing. In Sierra Leone we don't have good roads or proper electricity, and corruption is almost sinking us. Even in my own office the differences are obvious: the director of our organisation earns only $80 a month, whereas a person doing the same job in a Western country might earn thirty or forty times that amount. We haven't got the infrastructure we need to run the organisation efficiently. When I was in the Netherlands I visited youth agencies whose offices were better equipped than government offices in this country.

Issues like globalisation and sustainable development affect the lives of Africans daily; for us they are a matter of life and death. Many conferences have been convened, a lot of planning has taken place, but very little practical work has been done. It's time to make real changes that will improve the lives of the people of Africa, especially women and children. It's time to do practical work that will help transform people's lives for the better.

Ibrahim Alex Bangura

2. One planet

The Earth is our home. And we'd better look after it because it's the only home we've got. Scientists are investigating the prospect of making other planets habitable; some have even suggested that we may eventually be able to emigrate en masse to Mars. But that is unlikely to be practical for millennia, if ever. Besides, the prospects of making Mars habitable do not look good if we ruin the planet on which we evolved.

For the foreseeable future our wellbeing, and indeed our survival, will depend on the health of the terrestrial environment. Our food supply depends on our agricultural lands. Our oxygen depends on the Earth's oceans and forests. Any major disruption to the natural systems of the Earth could threaten our survival.

Yet the Earth's natural systems are under threat. Every year the world is losing 24 billion tonnes of topsoil and an area of forest the size of England and Wales. More than half the world's seventeen major fishing grounds have been severely depleted by over-fishing. In 2001 a UN committee predicted that global temperatures could rise by up to 5.8°C by 2100 — the largest climate change in more than 10000 years. Extreme weather events such as droughts and floods are likely to become more frequent in many parts of the world. There is a risk that global warming could release vast amounts of natural greenhouse gases into the atmosphere, creating a vicious circle that, in the words of Britain's Environment Minister Michael Meacher, could 'make our planet uninhabitable'.

Why are we faced with this environmental crisis? Why are we mistreating the Earth? Part of the answer is that we have lost touch with the natural world, both physically and spiritually. Many of us, particularly in the developed world, spend the greater part of our lives in artificial environments. We hardly ever see stars at night or hear the sound of wind in trees. Our food comes to us in packets and tins, and our rubbish is spirited away in trucks. We seldom pause to remind ourselves that everything we do affects our physical environment, be it driving a car, flicking a switch or filling a supermarket trolley.

Technology, too, has helped create the illusion that we are separate from the natural world and that we can control it to suit our convenience. We can insert human genes into pigs and, to some extent, we can even manipulate the weather (by cloud seeding). But technology cannot replace a billion tonnes of topsoil or restore the intricate diversity of a tropical rainforest once it has been cleared for grazing. We can't eradicate an engineered gene once it has escaped into the natural environment.

Humanity's alienation from the natural world is comparatively recent. Our human and hominoid ancestors lived in nature (and indeed were part of nature) for millions of years. By contrast, it is only ten thousand years since humans started using agriculture, and it is only in the last few centuries that a substantial proportion of the world's population has lived in cities and towns. Our bodies still resonate with the tides and we still breathe the oxygen that trees exhale. Even the most citified of us have some sense of being connected to nature. Why else would advertisers use images of mountain streams to sell us beer, and tropical beaches to sell us airline tickets?

We need to re-establish and strengthen the links that connect us to the Earth. One way we can do this is by redesigning our cities to let the natural world back in. In 2002 the city authorities of Tokyo, a treeless city, passed a law requiring all new major buildings to incorporate roof gardens. The additional greenery (potentially up to 30 square kilometres of it) will cool the city in summer, improve air quality and bring the beauty of living things into people's workaday lives.

We need to educate our children to understand what impact they will have on the environment when they drive a car, catch a plane or fill their homes with consumer items. We need to get out of our cities every once in a while and reconnect with the rivers and hills. Everyone should come into contact with wilderness at least once in their life – preferably when they are young – to allow them to see that nature has its own innate order and that there is a realm of creation beyond the world of human affairs.

The Earth is our home, but it is also the home of millions of other species. They, too, have the right to exist and to live out their own destinies. While our radio telescopes scan the heavens for signs of intelligent life, we tend to disregard the immense intelligence that has enabled life to thrive on Earth for the past four billion years. Every living creature has its own way of life and its own form of consciousness. We might think we are superior, but humanity is only one branch of a vast and immensely intricate tree.

The Earth is a living being. She has no nationality. She nurtures and sustains us, and all terrestrial life. She is not an investment opportunity or a toxic waste disposal site. She is not a resource to be used up and discarded as we move on to colonise other planets.

When we walk on the Earth, we walk on sacred ground.

The fight for the forests

Jill Redwood

EAST GIPPSLAND, AUSTRALIA

I have always loved the natural world and I've loved spending time alone with it. When other children were playing in the street I'd be off climbing a tree or playing with toy farmyard animals. When I was three or four my mother and I were having tea in our Melbourne backyard and ants were getting the sugar on the biscuits. I was squashing them with my finger. My mother said, 'Don't do that, they work really hard to get their food'. At that moment it clicked that they were sentient beings. *They're like me, they're like us!* So I crushed my biscuit and gave it to them. Since then I've seen every living creature as having feelings.

When I left school I knew I wanted to work with nature but had no idea how. My first job was in a laboratory where horrific animal experiments were being conducted. I tried to make the animals' lives a bit easier by giving them torn-up newspaper to play with and nest in, instead of them just pacing their cages. Later I worked for an agrochemical company, which at least got me out into the open air and working with plants. But it was several years before I bought land here in southeastern Victoria and my farmyard animals became a reality.

I've been involved in environmental and animal-welfare issues all my life, and when I moved to this region I became increasingly alarmed by what was happening to the forests. The East Gippsland area contains the most diverse range of temperate-forest ecosystems on Earth, and its magnificent eucalypt forests and rainforests are home to over 300 rare and threatened species. But only a fraction of these forests were protected, and the rest were being cut down at the rate of 15 football fields every day. I'd drive through areas that were staggeringly beautiful, and a few months later I'd go back and see massive bleeding holes in the bush where there used to be towering trees and carpets of ferns. I'd go for horse rides, and discover that whole mountainsides of forests had been wiped out. Forests with high conservation value were being clearfelled and replaced with plantations that would be cut down every 20 or 30 years. Our beautiful diverse forests were being turned into single-species woodchip farms.

In the early 1980s I joined a local group that opposed a pulp-mill development. The group,

called Concerned Residents of East Gippsland, was low-key and didn't have much influence. I started to make suggestions like, 'Why don't we get a logo?' and 'Why don't we have a newsletter?' These things never seemed to happen so I designed a logo myself and started a newsletter, which has been going for twelve years now. Then the people who started the group moved away and I was left holding the reins.

At first we were reasonable and polite – and we achieved absolutely nothing. So we started to use more controversial tactics such as exposing the mismanagement and economic insanity of the logging industry. On one occasion we obtained a leaked document that revealed the government was selling public forests to the woodchippers at less than $3 a log-truck load. That caused quite a stir when we released it to the media.

Over the years we've tried every conceivable nonviolent tactic to protect the forests in our area. We've lobbied politicians and run education campaigns. We discovered the region's biggest tree and invited celebrities to be photographed hugging its buttress; the tree is now in a protected area. We've run forest tours, organised rallies in Melbourne and made submissions to public inquiries. An expert on threatened species taught me how to carry out animal surveys, and since then we've done our own surveys in critically important areas. We've put out media releases at every possible opportunity; but of course, the logging industry's media releases always get the front page and ours get page 17 under the girls' hockey scores!

In the summer of 1988/89 we were in the middle of a major forest campaign when we heard about a proposal to put a 'very fast train' (VFT) through the mountains of East Gippsland. The development would have created a biological Berlin Wall through the region, and with thirty trains roaring through daily at 110 decibels our valley would have become uninhabitable. To make matters worse, the rail line would have gone right through my house!

'The government was selling public forests at less than $3 a log-truck load.'

Many local people were opposed to the development, but most of them were afraid to speak out because they didn't want to be seen associating with 'greenies'. So it was left to people like me to do all the work and to be ridiculed as 'anti-progress'. We started a new group and investigated the likely benefits and disadvantages of the VFT. We concluded that the project was unlikely to be economically viable without massive government subsidies; its main 'advantage' appeared to be that it would allow a consortium of companies to forcibly acquire huge areas of cheap land for development.

I spent two years fighting the VFT, all the while still working on the forest campaign. I'd often start work at 5 a.m. and would still be up writing media releases at 2 a.m. the following day. I was living in constant crisis mode. Eventually the VFT was killed off by a government inquiry; but I'm still spending 70 percent of my time working on the forest issue. This is not my idea of pleasant country living – I didn't come here to live like this. I'd much rather be doing creative things like weaving, training Clydesdale horses and working in the ecotourism business. But it's a battle that never ends.

For me, one of the hardest things about being an activist has been putting up with endless vilification and harassment. Recently a local newspaper printed a libellous letter about me, but it would have cost me thousands of dollars to take the paper to court. I've had severed goat's heads left in my letterbox and smashed bottles embedded in my driveway. I've had abusive phone calls late at night; I've even had a death threat. During the VFT campaign a reporter compiled a dossier on me and sent copies to the police and to local politicians. It was full of blatant lies, such as claiming I had a stash of machine-guns and was growing marijuana. Our local MP read out sections of it in parliament, and I had no recourse because he was speaking under parliamentary privilege. So those lies are now indelibly recorded in Australia's history. Years later, I found out that the Australian Police had notified Scotland Yard when I went on holiday to Britain, warning them that I was going there to study bombing techniques!

But the worst thing was that someone shot my Clydesdale. I'd had him since he was a foal and I'd trained him to work in harness by voice command alone. I didn't know how to ride a horse and he didn't know how to be ridden, but we worked it out together and I never fell off him. He was such a character; when I was outside playing the flute he used to rest his big head on my shoulder.

In the midst of all this conflict I occasionally get time to enjoy my farm and animals. I'm almost self-sufficient in food and I make a bit of money drawing cartoons and writing for a magazine. I've also built a solar-powered tourist cottage using environmentally friendly materials. It gives visitors the opportunity to experience a sustainable living space.

During the past few years I've been getting more and more phone calls from loggers who are unhappy about what's happening in the forests. Some of them are prepared to speak out, so we've started a community group that includes loggers and conservationists. We've put up a proposal for a 300-kilometre tourist walk as an economic alternative for the East Gippsland region, and we've got the large woodchipping interests quite worried. I'm currently running as a Greens candidate for the local council under the slogan 'Vote Redwood to clear out the deadwood'!

What has all this effort achieved? So far, very little. There's one area that we fought a seven-year battle for, and I can die half-happy knowing that it's safe forever. But when the government protected it they gave other reserved areas back to the loggers. Perhaps things would be worse if conservationists weren't there – and that's really the best I can console myself with.

I suppose I was born with a strong streak of stubbornness; or maybe it's just a hatred of injustice. I feel compelled to protect things that can't speak for themselves. I can't put blinkers on and ignore the lies and the legalised vandalism, just because the government says it's okay. In years to come, people will realise that the fight for the forests was as necessary as the fights to stop slavery and whaling. We keep fighting in the hope that we can save what's left. One day we will be vindicated.

Jill Redwood

3. Responsibility

Each of us bears a share of responsibility for our communities, and hence for the world as a whole.

Everything we do affects the world around us. If we pour chemicals down the sink we damage our rivers. When we burn fossil fuels we contribute to the pressure on the world's climatic systems. The way we vote (if we have the opportunity to vote) affects the political climate of the societies in which we live. The simple act of buying a shirt – or deciding not to buy one – can affect the lives of people living halfway around the world.

Each of us contributes to the culture of our communities, and hence to the culture of all humanity – 'culture' not just in the sense of what music we listen to or which holidays we celebrate, but the totality of the way we relate to one another. If we are peaceful in ourselves and in our daily lives, we contribute to peace around the world. If we are jingoistic, subscribing to the ideology of 'us' and 'them', we help to maintain the divisions that ultimately lead to war.

After the 1982 Falklands War, a British woman whose son had been killed was interviewed on television. Asked if she thought her son's death had been necessary, she replied, 'Perhaps, for Britain's sake … '. She didn't realise that by her patriotic sentiments, she herself had helped to cause the war that killed her son.

It may *seem* that we have little influence over the forces that affect our lives. Our armies may be sent to war at the whim of vote-hungry politicians or their corporate sponsors (such as oil companies and arms manufacturers). Our stock markets may crash because of the actions of speculators who never have to face an election. But the power structures and institutions that shape our world have not come into existence by some mysterious chance. They have been created, and they are maintained, with our cooperation. The corporate world has become all-powerful because our culture worships money and applauds the pursuit of profit and power. The armaments industry is thriving because most of our governments are willing to resort to violence when our so-called national interests appear to be under threat.

Few of us become cabinet ministers or corporate executives. But we are all faced with the everyday challenges of relationship – to other people, to the Earth and to our own thoughts and feelings. Relationship is the foundation on which society is built; it is the fundamental element on which everything depends. If we are aggressive in our daily lives, no political system can create a peaceful society. If we are materialistic and greedy, no amount of economic growth will narrow the gap between rich and poor.

Those of us who are not caught in a daily struggle for survival have the opportunity to explore the challenges of relationship in our own lives. Indeed, we have a *responsibility* to explore these challenges, because the way we meet them is vitally important for the wellbeing of humanity. We can't leave it to politicians to solve the world's problems – the insecurity of the human psyche cannot be resolved by politics. We can't leave it to 'the experts' because we ourselves have to change.

We are responsible for both the consequences of our actions and the consequences of our failure to act. We cannot justify inaction by arguing that the future is uncertain. We can never be sure what the future will bring or whether our efforts to change will succeed. All we can know for certain is that change is inevitable, because we can't go on living the way we are. Either we seize the initiative to change, or the tide of change will sweep us away.

Everything we do, however small, affects the world around us. Our words, our gestures, our facial expressions, the way we look at other people – all these affect our relationships and the cultural environment in which we live. Words that you say today may stay with someone for the rest of their life. Even our thoughts affect the world; indeed, *especially* our thoughts, because our thoughts inform and influence everything we do.

On a trip to India in 1983 I encountered a young girl selling newspapers amid the bustle and dirt of a Delhi street. She looked up at me – and her smile filled the world. Twenty years later, I can still feel the radiance of that smile.

If you are courteous to someone in the street you can lift that person's spirits, giving them the strength of heart to face their problems and to be courteous to someone else. It is like a wave travelling outwards, ultimately across the world. A harsh word adds a brick to humanity's burden of unhappiness.

Denting the sword

Angie Zelter

UNITED KINGDOM/PALESTINE

In 1996 I was one of a group of ten women who disabled a Hawk jet that was earmarked for sale to the Indonesian military. Three of the group broke into the British Aerospace hangar in northern England and damaged the plane's fuselage and electronics with hammers before giving themselves up to the police. I was arrested two days later after announcing my intention to commit similar actions, and the four of us spent six months in jail awaiting trial.

When the case was heard, we argued that we had acted to prevent the greater crime of genocide, because jets like these were being used against civilians in East Timor. To support our claim we showed a video that we'd made and left at the scene of the 'crime', which included eyewitness accounts by people in East Timor. Nobel Peace Prize winner Jose Ramos Horta and journalist John Pilger were among those who gave evidence in our defence. The jury accepted our arguments and we were acquitted, against the advice of the judge.

Three years later a group of us achieved a more significant legal breakthrough following an action in which we damaged a research laboratory that plays a key role in Britain's Trident submarine nuclear-defence system. On that occasion the judge accepted our argument that Britain's deployment of nuclear weapons contravenes international law. We cited a range of legal precedents including a 1996 opinion by the International Court of Justice, which ruled that states should never make civilians the object of attack and must never use weapons that are incapable of distinguishing between civilian and military targets. Each of a Trident submarine's 48 nuclear warheads is eight times more powerful than the Hiroshima bomb, and its use would inevitably cause massive civilian casualties. Judge Gimblett's decision caused a major stir in legal and political circles; the government referred it to the High Court for review. Although the High Court ruled that our actions were unlawful, it did not have the power to overturn our acquittal, and the trial allowed us to expose many of the flaws and hypocrisies in the government's arguments.

For me, the downside of the Hawk jet action was that it put a small group of us on a pedestal, and there were no actions to follow it up. Few people are willing to risk years in jail, and I felt that

if the disarmament campaign was to be effective, it needed to have large numbers of people involved over a long period of time. For this to happen there needed to be some kind of structure, and this led me to found Trident Ploughshares in 1998. Members of Trident Ploughshares take part in a variety of nonviolent, open and accountable actions designed to hinder the working of the Trident system. These actions range from blockades to fence-cutting to actually disarming parts of the Trident system.

In court we have consistently argued that our actions are necessary because we have exhausted all other reasonable avenues for persuading the government to abandon nuclear weapons. Our website contains a wealth of evidence in support of this claim, including records of our dialogue with the government over a period of several years. Since the formation of Trident Ploughshares, our members have taken part in dozens of actions that have substantially raised the profile of the nuclear weapons debate – particularly in Scotland, where 85 percent of the public are opposed to the presence of nuclear weapons on Scottish soil. We've received expressions of support from hundreds of community leaders including the Mayor of London, the Archbishop of Canterbury and the American academic Noam Chomsky.

There will always be people who say that what we are doing is irresponsible or that we are encouraging anarchy. We argue that when a government acts illegally by setting up the apparatus for war crimes on an unimaginable scale, citizens have a right – and indeed a responsibility –

to intervene. We go to great lengths to ensure that our actions pose no threat to human life or limb. Everyone who takes part in Trident Ploughshares' actions is required to undergo intense nonviolence training. If we damage anything, we invariably give ourselves up to the police and explain exactly what damage we've done. Of course there is an element of personal risk in what we do, but this is minimal compared to the risk of nuclear weapons being used in war or detonated by terrorists or human error.

I have always felt that a part of life is service, that we are not just here for our own selfish ends. But it was not until I was in my final year of university that I began to realise what was going on in the world. A turning point for me was picking up the first issue of *The Ecologist*, which included an overview of all the major crises that were facing us – from poverty to global warming to nuclear weapons to species loss. For all my so-called education, I knew nothing about the real issues that were affecting the world.

'When a government acts illegally citizens have a responsibility to intervene.'

After I left university my husband and I spent three years doing development work in Cameroon. For the first time I came across racial prejudice directly, and I realised that colonialism is far from dead. We threw a party a few months after we'd arrived, and racial segregation occurred right there in my living room. All of the whites were standing at one end of the room and all of the blacks were at the other, the women were on one side, the men on the other, and I was standing helplessly in the middle. I began to wonder what I was doing in Africa and to question the whole idea of Western-style 'development'. Many locals told me that if I wanted to help Africa I should go back to the West and change policies there, because that's where most of Africa's problems originated.

I arrived back in Britain with a young child and my second about to be born. The West was in the grip of the Cold War and it was clear to me that the major issue facing Britain at that time was how not to blow up the rest of the world. That's when I began to get involved in the peace movement, particularly in the campaign against Britain's weapons of mass destruction. I also became heavily involved in forest issues and in the ultimately successful campaign to persuade several British companies to buy timber only from sustainable sources. I've always been a grassroots campaigner and a strong advocate of nonviolent civil disobedience. I've been arrested over a hundred times in seven countries and I've spent a total of 20 months in jail.

Recently I've become increasingly involved in the peace movement in Palestine, and I'm currently participating in a three-year project involving an international team of sixteen women based in the village of Hares in the West Bank. I have a personal connection with Israel because I married into a Jewish family; at one stage my son considered settling there and might have been called up for military service. I've also been interested in the Middle East situation for many years because Israel was built out of the ashes of the Holocaust. I've pondered long and hard on how ordinary, loving human beings could have participated in such terrible things, and how the victim so often becomes the oppressor. I think a large part of the 'how' is the ease with which most people obey authority and turn over their own responsibility to others.

I think living morally is actually quite simple: you just have to love people. If everybody treated each other as respected and well-loved friends we wouldn't have things like weapons of mass destruction or the repression of the Palestinian people. This may sound idealistic but it's really very simple and practical. When I was attacked by Israeli settlers in October 2002 I was able to see them as human beings. As soon as I was able to establish eye contact with one of them and show him that I wasn't a threat, he calmed down. We ended up talking for about 45 minutes. Most people want to do good; it all depends on what you bring out in them.

The complexity that we have to put into our political campaigns and legal challenges is unnecessary, really. We don't need any more knowledge about what's wrong; we simply have to act upon it. The problem is that people aren't willing to act and take personal responsibility for what happens. It's simple, but we make it complex because we don't want to bear the consequences of love in action.

I constantly question what I am doing and whether activism is the best response to what's happening in the world. If I forgot all about being an activist and just lived fully in the moment, with real love for the people around me, maybe that would be enough. I question whether the structures we build to fight violence and oppression aren't really part of the same thing – as you fight the enemy you become like the enemy. The only way through that is to be aware that good ends do not justify evil means; the means must always be consistent with the ends. If you put evil into your daily life or into the structures that you build, then you are going to reap that evil. So you have to be very, very careful.

Angie Zelter

4. Making a difference

Many of us are concerned about the state of the world, but feel there's not much we can do. The media bring us daily reports of wars, suffering, corruption and environmental problems, but they rarely bring us stories of positive change. It's easy to feel overwhelmed, and it's easy to use this feeling as an excuse for doing nothing. The world is a vast place – what can one person do?

It is incredible what one person can do. In 1995 a young Canadian called Craig Kielburger set up an international youth-run organisation called Free The Children to help the victims of child labour in developing countries. His efforts attracted the attention of presidents, prime ministers, monarchs and popes, and Free The Children now has more than 100 000 members in 35 countries. In 1995 Craig Kielburger was just twelve years old. The Indian activist Jaya Arunachalam has helped tens of thousands of women in the slums of southeast India to agitate for better wages and an end to the dowry system. Seeing the need for reforestation in the Himalayan foothills, Visheswar Saklani started planting trees himself – and planted 200 000 of them. Individuals like Mohandas Gandhi and Nelson Mandela have changed the course of history in their own countries and beyond.

It is tempting to say that these people are exceptional – implying that, since we are not exceptional, we could never aspire to such achievements. But is that true? Certainly these people are to be admired – not least because they took a stand on something that they felt demanded action. And that's something all of us can do.

It is incredible what people can accomplish when they combine their talents and energies. When Australia's fledgling Wilderness Society launched its campaign to save the Franklin River in Tasmania's southwest wilderness, its command centre consisted of a single desk. At that time (1976) the proposal to dam the Franklin was supported by both major parties in the Tasmanian state and the Australian federal parliaments, by powerful industry lobby groups and unions, and by a majority of Tasmanian citizens. After seven years, more than a thousand arrests and a national election in which the fate of the river played a significant role, the Franklin River was protected.

The Tasmanian authorities later conceded that the dam wasn't required.

You don't have to be famous to make a difference in the world. Individuals like Nelson Mandela and organisations like the Wilderness Society could not have achieved their successes without the support and hard work of thousands of like-minded people. Many of these people work for years doing unglamorous tasks such as writing media releases, organising meetings or simply doing office chores. They may remain unknown outside their immediate circles of friends and colleagues, but they contribute enormously to making the world a better place.

You don't have to be an activist. The problems that confront us are not just political in nature; they reflect deep conflicts in the way we relate to one another and to the Earth. Addressing these conflicts requires not only social and political change, but also a fundamental change in our awareness and understanding.

You can help to bring this change about in your work, in your relationships and in your daily life. You can change the way you eat, the way you talk, the way you think and the way you spend money. You can try your hand at writing a book, or set off around the world in search of the truth that lies within you. In a world where so much is being sacrificed for short-term and superficial gains, you can challenge the status quo by making something that will last a hundred years or by doing something simply for the joy of it.

You can change your video-viewing habits – for example, by making your own documentary videos. Roberto Arévalo teaches teenagers in Boston to do just that. An immigrant from Colombia, Arévalo supported himself as a labourer while studying media communications. Hired in 1992 to make videos about substance-abuse prevention programs, he encouraged city teenagers to make documentaries about their neighbourhoods and communities. Work by Arévalo's students has been widely exhibited in the United States, and his 'Mirror Project' has been recognised as one of the nation's most successful art programs for at-risk youth.

As an individual you have the opportunity to think for yourself – and that is an immensely valuable gift. We tend to accept what we are told by our teachers, priests and political leaders; we buy what we are persuaded to buy, ideologically or otherwise. Increasingly, governments are relying on marketing experts and public relations campaigns to garner support for their agendas; it is a form of mind control. On the day in 1991 that Britain's former Prime Minister Margaret Thatcher stepped down from office, she knighted the head of her public relations firm.

If we thought for ourselves we might see through the lies of politicians and the glossy deceptions of advertisers. We might question the credibility of mainstream economists whose definition of a 'healthy' economy ignores human and ecological wellbeing. We might question the justice of exploiting the citizens of developing countries, only to slam a door in their face when they try to emigrate to the West. We might question whether we

need the fancy house, the latest-model car and the thirty-year bank loan that we've been led to believe are essential for our happiness.

Everything we do affects the world around us. If we can learn to live happily, we will contribute to humanity's understanding of the art of living happily. If we can live sanely, we will create islands of sanity amid the confusion of the world. Our sanity and happiness will inevitably have an effect, like ripples from a stone dropped into a pond. And if enough people change, the ripples can become a flood.

The writing on the wall

Rowenna Davis

LONDON, UK

I was sitting on a train, thinking 'It's the year 2000 and I'm fifteen years old. What have I got to show for my life?' A billboard caught my eye and I thought, 'Wouldn't it be great to put up posters that made people think about the state of the world?' There was so much advertising space in London, and most of it was being used to persuade people to keep consuming. If I could get people to stop and think, even for one minute, maybe that would make a difference.

Then I thought, 'Why don't I do something big? Look at Joan of Arc – she had done so much by the time she was fifteen. I can do more than I'm doing now.' I thought about putting up a thousand posters, but they would have been lost in a place the size of London. Why not put up ten thousand posters? Was it possible? Could I afford them? Ten thousand came to be a sort of dream figure, and it was the figure I eventually decided upon for the 'Messengers' campaign.

It was only much later that I remembered I'd done something similar years before. When I was seven I'd been fed up with all the litter in my street, so I'd got on my father's computer, designed an anti-littering poster and printed off a hundred of them. Then I coloured them in, decorated them with glitter and put one in every letterbox in my block. I can't remember if the street got any cleaner, but there's no litter in it now!

I didn't tell anyone about my plans for the new campaign except my brother Robert and my best friend, Melissa Manteghi. Melissa designed the posters and the success of the campaign owes much to her artistic skills. She had faith in the project right from the start; she is the sort of person who believes anything is possible. I remember her saying, 'It's not just the government that has to change things; it's the people as well. After all, the government doesn't force you to drive to work in the morning. The campaign might inspire people in the smallest way, but this can have a cumulative effect.'

For the next year and a half I saved money by babysitting, tutoring, walking everywhere and shopping in car boot sales. Literally every pound that I earned went straight into my bank account. It was hard for my family at Christmas because I had to tell them, 'Sorry, I'll be making all your presents this year!' But I didn't feel as if I was missing out on anything. I'm in a situation where I've

got everything I need. In fact I feel a bit guilty living in England, because we are so fortunate compared to most of the world. I often hear my friends saying, 'I can't do such-and-such because I haven't got enough money'. It's so nice to feel liberated from that.

When I'd saved nearly £1000 ($US 1560) I started investigating printing costs. I discovered that it was going to cost twice as much to get the posters printed in an environmentally friendly way. So I thought, 'Right, I'm going to have to save up a bit more, then!' Meanwhile I heard about the forthcoming Earth Summit in Johannesburg, and it occurred to me that the Messengers campaign would be an excellent way to publicise the issues that were going to be discussed there. I decided to print ten versions of the poster, each with a statement that related to one of the summit's main themes. One poster had the message, 'One quarter of all people don't have water today'; another read, '25% of the world's animals and 11% of its birds are at risk of extinction'. I selected the statements carefully after trawling through numerous UN reports and double-checking the information sources. I wanted them to be representative, not the most extreme facts I could find.

When the time came to withdraw all my money from the bank – more than £2000 – I didn't even think to take a bag to put it in. I sat on the Tube with my pockets bulging, thinking 'Oh my God, what have I done?' At the printers I

'I'm fifteen years old. took the money out bit by bit – 'Here's some … here's a bit more …'. They looked at me as if I'd robbed a bank. My parents knew nothing

What have I got to about what I'd been doing until a van pulled up outside my mother's house and delivered a pile of posters that was taller than I am. Then I

show for my life?' went to school and handed out leaflets to all my friends, explaining what I was doing and saying, 'Come to Speakers' Corner in Hyde Park on the evening of July 24 and bring as many friends as you can. Work

in pairs and dress in black.' I also rang practically everyone I'd ever met and asked them to come along. I wanted to get all the posters up on a single night, partly because the police would have stopped us during the day and partly because I liked the idea of people all over London waking up and wondering, 'Where have all these messages come from?'

After spending most of July 24 sending out press releases, I loaded up my mother's car in the evening and she drove me to Speakers' Corner. There was nowhere to park so I had to bundle out all the posters, buckets, glue, containers of water (to mix up the glue), brushes, maps and bus timetables onto the pavement while curious tourists looked on. I had no idea whether anything else would be happening at Speakers' Corner, whether I'd have enough water or glue, how illegal the whole thing was, or whether the police would have been tipped off. I was sure that some of my friends would come but I didn't know if I'd have enough people. In the end more than a hundred people came, almost all under eighteen. It was such a good feeling because race or class or gender didn't matter; we were just a bunch of young people getting together because we believed in something. It countered a lot of the ideas people have about young people being apathetic.

By 11 p.m. most of the posters were already up, so my own group went off to put some up in areas where no-one else had wanted to go. We were still going at sunrise. The police stopped a couple of our people that night and asked them not to put up any more, but as soon as the police left they just kept going. Only one person was arrested, and when she explained what she was doing the police were so impressed they put posters up all over the police station! In the morning I went home and slept for an hour, then went around asking shopkeepers to put the posters up in their windows. Late in the afternoon I caught a bus up to Oxford Street, and there were posters *everywhere*!

The night's operation had been a success. One person had put up a continuous line of posters in Trafalgar Square. I managed to paste one every five paces along the pavement on Waterloo Bridge. When I checked my email there was a message from the Department of Public Transport saying, 'We've had phone calls from 250 bus stops all over London with your posters on them. We're going to have to hire special cleaning crews to get them off!' I replied with an apology, because obviously Public Transport aren't the sort of people I'd want to annoy. I said I'd be happy to pay for their removal or help take them down, but they said, 'No, it's okay. Actually we agree with what you are doing. Just make sure that next time you don't use PVA glue, because it doesn't come off!'

For quite a while that was the only email I got, and the media coverage was quite disappointing. Then more than 500 emails came in, all of them positive and many of them from visiting tourists. Two were from people who wanted to start their own poster campaigns. *Face* magazine ran a story on the campaign and I was interviewed by the BBC. Partly because of the Messengers campaign I won a scholarship to travel to South Africa, where I attended the Children's Earth Summit and was invited to meet the main summit's British delegation.

Some people think that what I did was self-sacrificing, but I've got far more out of it than I ever put in. The trip to South Africa alone was worth more than the posters, so the campaign was actually good value for money! I know people who've spent £1000 on computer games; they do it because computer games are fun, you can play them with your friends and they give you a reason to get out of bed on a Saturday morning. I did the Messengers campaign for exactly the same reasons. The time I spent saving money for the campaign was one of the happiest times of my life.

I'm not sure what I'll do next. Right now I'm focusing on passing my A levels. I've also decided to buy my school a set of solar panels. That's £3500 away at the moment, but I've already saved almost £1000.

Rowenna Davis

Principles
of
Awareness

5. Learning

Living requires constant learning, and questioning can help free our minds to learn.

To live responsibly and sanely we must be prepared to learn, not only while we are at school or university but every day of our lives. The word 'learning' generally means acquiring knowledge, ideas and skills; but in a broader sense learning implies being open to new ways of perceiving and understanding life. Knowledge and ideas are obviously necessary, but they can also be barriers to understanding. Life is constantly throwing up new challenges, and if we respond to these challenges with fixed ideas we will be incapable of meeting them.

Most of us have difficulty meeting life anew because our minds are burdened with preconceptions. We are conditioned from an early age to accept a particular set of beliefs, and we rarely if ever question them – let alone question whether we need beliefs at all. People who grow up in overtly Christian cultures tend to accept Christian values and beliefs; the same is true for every culture. Even if we question the belief-systems of our mother culture, we all too easily get caught up in other systems or in the 'culture' of our own ideas and conclusions. Young people may reject the values of their parents and teachers – only to adopt the beliefs and conventions of the latest counterculture.

You may think your beliefs are right — and that could be part of the problem. Most of us go around convinced that we are right, seeing only what we want to see, hearing what we want to hear. The conviction that we are right can prevent us from appreciating the limitations of our beliefs and from listening to alternatives. A belief may be 'right' as far as it goes; but all beliefs are limited because they are mental formulations based on experience. Like maps, such formulations can be a useful guide; but, like maps, they have limited accuracy and scope, and need to be periodically revised if they are to remain useful. Unlike maps, however, our beliefs are often prejudiced by fears and desires that we may or may not be consciously aware of. I may subscribe to a particular religion, for example, because I am afraid of death or because my ego is attracted to the idea of being one of God's 'chosen few'.

Unquestioned beliefs are one of the primary causes of conflict in the world, and one of the primary obstacles to conflict resolution. In regions like the Middle East, Kashmir and Northern Ireland, people have been indoctrinated for centuries in the name of religion. The resulting divisions have caused tens of thousands of violent deaths. In 2002 a survey in Belfast revealed that two-thirds of young adults living in housing estates near the so-called 'peace lines' had never had a meaningful conversation with anyone from the 'other' side. Religions and political ideologies may claim to unite humanity, but when they encourage unquestioning belief, they sow seeds of factionalism and hostility.

Beliefs give us a sense of security, not only physically but also psychologically. It is reassuring to feel that we know who we are, why we are here, where we are going and how we should act. But this sense of security is deceptive, because the more rigidly we cling to our beliefs, the less clearly we can see how things actually are; and the less clearly we see,

the less intelligent our responses will be. To be receptive to life our minds need
to be flexible, like blades of grass in a storm. When a storm comes, a tree may be broken
but a blade of grass survives.

One way to keep our minds flexible is by asking radical questions – radical in the sense of
digging down deep (from the Latin 'radix', meaning 'root'). Why do we hold a particular
belief? What is property, and what can we rightfully call our own? What is implied in
living sustainably? What are the ethical implications of genetic engineering? What is
anger? Is it possible to live without violence? Deep down, what are we really seeking in
life? The exploration of such questions can deepen our understanding and expose the
provisional nature of beliefs we thought were certainties.

Radical questions are unlikely to have immediate answers, and indeed may not have
answers at all in the usual sense of the word. The purpose of asking radical questions is
not to arrive at conclusions, but rather to put conclusions aside and undertake a journey
of inquiry. If we regard questions not as interrogations but as probes, we can use them
to explore realms of insight that lie beyond our certainties.

Silence, too, has a role to play in serious inquiry. Most of the verbal exchanges that take
place in our society allow very little space for silence. When someone asks you a question,
you usually feel obliged to give some sort of response before they get impatient with you.
But silence may be the best response if the question you have been asked is deeply
challenging, because it allows time for the question to sink into your mind.

A deeply challenging question can stop your conscious mind in its tracks: you simply don't
know what the answer is, or even how to go about finding the answer. If you start
speculating or quoting someone else, you are only avoiding the fact that you have reached
the limit of your understanding. By remaining silent you accept this fact, the very realisation
of which can bring a deeper understanding. Outwardly it may appear that the conversation

has run out of energy. But it is precisely in moments like these – when the upper, verbalising levels of the brain are temporarily in abeyance – that deep learning can take place.

We tend to avoid asking radical questions because they bring us face to face with uncertainty. But is uncertainty such a bad thing? Uncertainty can appear threatening if, out of fear, we cling to the 'certainty' of our ideas and conclusions. When we see that this certainty is misplaced, we are faced with the fact that life is a moment-by-moment journey into the unknown. Then uncertainty is not something to be feared, but a creative state in which we can learn.

Learning in freedom

Venu

BANGALORE, INDIA

At the Centre for Learning (CFL), in southern India, we are trying to create an environment where children and adults can learn together in freedom. Humanity is on the brink of several disasters and it seems clear to us that the challenges we face, whether at the personal or global level, are not amenable to simple technical solutions. By and large, education is failing to meet these challenges because it focuses almost exclusively on skills and is preparing the young to compete in a culture that values achievement and success at the expense of nature and community. As educators, our primary concern is to awaken – both in the student and in ourselves – a creative awareness that is capable of examining and moving beyond the barriers to relationship. We share a deep interest in the work of J. Krishnamurti, who suggested that education has a central role to play in nurturing this kind of awareness.

At CFL we do not have a 'system' of education because learning, by its very nature, is fluid, and when you systematise something you tend to make it inflexible. Nor do the staff assume a position of authority in relation to the students, because in the field of self-learning the teacher cannot claim to know a truth that he or she can transmit to another. The school has no hierarchy, no principal and no single spokesperson. Even the intentions and the concerns of the school are not irrevocably fixed, but are open to questioning and revision. The students and teachers at CFL are participating together in an inward journey that is not dependent on any dogma or authority.

Having set aside authority, and in particular the authority of reward and punishment, we are faced with the question of how to foster a climate of responsibility. Very often an environment that denies authority can be assumed to be one that promises licence. So one of the themes that we pursue with the students is what it means to live responsibly, and whether there can be freedom in our relationships without it becoming a free-for-all. The small size and the open structure of the school make these questions immediate. The close contact between students of all ages helps younger students especially to understand the implications of responsibility in daily life.

We see dialogue as crucial for maintaining healthy relationships in the school. Indeed, we rely exclusively on dialogue when difficulties arise (as they inevitably do) and when decisions need to be made. We encourage students to participate in dialogue from a very young age. For us 'dialogue' is not merely an exchange of opinions and ideas; rather, it is a process in which we explore whether it is possible to 'see together' by moving beyond our personal opinions and conditioning. Naturally this is often difficult, but it becomes easier when there is an atmosphere of mutual affection and respect. It is crucial that those who participate in dialogue, particularly staff, have the capacity to understand their feelings and talk about them openly. For this reason, the staff meetings are often intense, and can seem quite raw to an outside observer. Anyone who walked into a 'Friday meeting' expecting a mild conversation could find it quite unnerving!

When we started CFL in 1990 we had no infrastructure and very little money. We just started with people and were determined not to let financial considerations be a deciding factor. In the first year we taught eight students in one of our homes; we moved many times in the next few years, using temporary structures like geodesic domes and thatched huts. We also made use of facilities in Bangalore such as libraries and public gardens. It was not until January 2000 that we moved onto our present (and permanent) campus, a twenty-acre block of very beautiful land about 45 km from Bangalore. The older children and many of the staff board here on weeknights, and younger students board here on Monday and Wednesday nights.

For the last few years CFL has had around 60 students and between fifteen and twenty staff, with an even gender mix. Most of the staff are university educated, although only a few of us trained as school teachers. We feel that 60 is about the right number of students because it means that the school is small enough for everyone to know each other on a personal basis. Although the school has a small number of maintenance staff, the staff and students share most of the everyday work such as cooking, cleaning and gardening. We charge parents fees according to what they can afford. Most of our students come from middle-class families, but low income would not be a barrier if we felt that a child was suitable for the school. We also offer informal classes to children from local villages, and give them access to facilities such as our library. Fees meet only 60 percent of the school's expenses, and the deficit is met by interest on a fund that we have built up largely through donations. We have always felt it important for the school to have an income independent of tuition fees, because schools that depend too heavily on fees usually end up either being very big or having excessively high fees.

The children here range in age from six to eighteen. For the younger children our focus is on fostering awareness and care of the body, and on developing sensitivity through exposure to nature, music, dance, craft and physical activity. The fundamentals of language and arithmetic are introduced with minimum pressure and, where possible, integrated with activities such as story-telling, cooking, drama, bird-watching, looking after pets, and play. As teachers, one of the questions we are exploring is how to nurture observation and awareness, given the brain's tendency to demand activity and to be constantly preoccupied with thought. Long walks in the countryside are part of the day, and these walks are often quiet – the emphasis is on observation, not on classification or recording. Many of the older students also take frequent walks in the surrounding forests and hills, as well as working on the land. A few lucky ones have spotted bears, jackals, a porcupine and even a panther.

'In twelve years I have never heard a student say that they did better or worse than someone else.'

With older students there is more emphasis on developing skills and helping students discover their interests. Our academic program helps the students develop greater knowledge, thinking and conceptual skills, and we encourage students to understand these in the context of their own lives and relationships. For example, in economics classes students are encouraged to relate what they are learning to the economic choices that they face in their lives.

At the end of their tenth year, students obtain the Cambridge IGCSE certification, and those who stay until the twelfth year take the International A levels. For younger students there are no exams and we have no comparative grading. We don't expect to abolish competitive behaviour simply by removing grading, but we feel that it is an important step in allowing students to discover values that go beyond mere achievement. The small class sizes help us to foster such values because they allow teachers to maintain personal contact with students and to assess their 'progress' without having to measure it on a scale of one to ten. In the twelve years that I have been with the school I have never heard a student say that they did better or worse than someone else.

In 1994 we introduced a Post School Programme in which a small number of students stay on and pursue undergraduate studies. We encourage these students to inquire into what constitutes 'right livelihood', and to find out whether it is possible to find happiness doing what one enjoys, even if it is not considered lucrative in today's society. The students have chosen areas of speciali-sation ranging from mathematics and international economics to design and writing.

There is a widespread belief that children need to learn to compete if they are to survive in a competitive world, but we haven't found this to be the case. On the contrary, we are convinced that when people love what they are doing and are confident in their talents, their confidence and love will see them through. Very often the fear of 'not surviving' is really the fear that one will fail to live up to society's expectations. When one is free of that fear, survival is not difficult. Some of our former students are working in art, craft, ecology and conservation, and we also have our quota of PhD students. Our academic standards are actually quite high. As far as I know, none of our former students feel that their ability to survive has been impaired because they are not sufficiently competitive.

Parents play a vital role in the life of CFL. Many parents are looking for an alternative to mainstream education, but we only accept parents who are deeply interested in what we are trying to do. To find out whether this is the case, we meet with the parents over an extended period. Once we accept a student, we invite the parents to participate in the ongoing dialogue about the school's intent and about the challenges that we face in life and relationship. We have day-long meetings every month where parents and teachers can explore these issues, and many parents also work here as volunteers.

There is no claim that CFL is a perfect environment or that we have a formula for awakening intelligence. We are simply a group of concerned individuals who have taken a difficult and uncertain path with all its travails. In my view, this is one of our strengths because it means that from one day to the next we are exploring anew the challenges of living and learning. This creates a certain sensitivity and a shared sense of looking afresh at the problems of relationship. Perhaps this very exploration, which is at once good-humoured and deeply serious, can awaken creativity and help to bring about a regeneration in society.

Venu

6. Seeing

Being aware means seeing with our hearts as well as our minds.

To be awake is to be aware: of light and darkness; of pleasure and pain; of the sounds from a nearby street; of the hesitation behind a smile. If we are vitally aware of the world around us, and of our own inner worlds, life can become an extraordinary journey, replete with beauty and mystery. If our awareness is impaired, our lives can become narrow and our ability to respond to the challenges of life can be severely limited.

Infants gaze with wonder at the everyday world. But as we get older our eyes can grow dim and our other senses can become muffled and dulled. The problem is not the deterioration of our physical senses, although this happens eventually, but rather a narrowing of the mental process of perception. The more we get used to things and preoccupied with the day-to-day affairs of our lives, the more we tend to see the world through a screen of tired familiarity. Living in an urban environment does not help because there is little in concrete walls and traffic jams to lift our spirits. When truth and beauty cross our path, we may not even be aware of them.

What does it mean to be aware? What is involved in seeing or hearing? What happens when you see a leaf, a factory or a photograph of starving children? These are fundamental questions but we seldom consider them. And that is extraordinary when you think about it. Everything we experience in life, we experience through the act of perception; yet we seldom pause to ask ourselves what this act involves.

What happens when you see a tree? Suppose you pass a tree as you are walking down the street. You may scarcely even notice it because your mind is filled with other things – catching a bus, humming a tune or recalling something you saw on TV. Your preoccupations make you insensitive to what is happening around you. You register the tree unconsciously so that you don't walk into it, but that is all. You may be totally unaware of a bird singing in the tree.

What happens if you look at the tree? You may say to yourself, 'That's a eucalypt' or 'That looks like the tree in my neighbour's garden'. If you do, you are interpreting the tree in terms of what you know. You may say, 'What a beautiful tree'; but the moment you say that, your mind has already wandered off into thought. A botanist might recognise signs that the tree is deficient in nutrients. A poet might sense the desolation of a living thing stranded in a desert of asphalt.

I once had a job that involved felling trees and splitting timber to stabilise walking tracks. After several months I found that whenever I looked at a tree, I would immediately start sizing it up for its timber potential. It had become an automatic reaction, even when I was walking for pleasure. I had to mentally step out of my 'timber-getter' role before I could see the trees for the wood.

You may wonder what seeing trees has to do with living responsibly in the world.

It is immediately relevant because if we are insensitive to our surroundings we will be unable to appreciate the beauty of life or understand the significance of what is happening in the world. Each of us approaches trees – and the world – with our own preconceptions and preoccupations, and these limit our ability to see trees or the world. If we are not sensitive to reality we won't be able to see anything clearly, because every tree and every situation – even every snowflake – is different. Life never repeats itself exactly.

If you can't see trees you won't be able to see human beings. The principles of perception are the same in either case. If I approach you with preconceptions and prejudices, can I see you as you really are? If my mind is wandering while you are talking, can I hope to understand you? If I want to hear what you are saying I have to really *listen* to you – which means my mind must be calm and receptive, not full of its own noise.

To be aware we need to see with our hearts as well as our minds. The advocates of economic rationalism and corporate-led 'progress' have denigrated the emotions of those who question their ideologies. They have branded liberals and conservationists as 'irrational' and 'emotional'. But the uncritical worship of profit and 'progress' is itself irrational; and if we lack feelings for each other and for the Earth we might as well be dead.

If you look at a tree with rational eyes you may see it only as an object, a resource or a scientific curiosity. If you look with affection, with wonder, with care, you may see something entirely different: a living being whose beauty and mystery can never be conveyed in words.

After all, what is a tree? What is it actually? We all 'know' what trees are in the sense that we have seen them before – or we think we have seen them. We have pictures in our minds with the caption 'Tree' attached. We can recognise various types of trees, and we have a certain amount of botanical knowledge about how trees develop, and so on. But none of

this is an actual tree. A tree is not the word 'tree'; nor is it our knowledge of a tree. A tree is not a scientific category, an image or a recognised form. However learned and subtle your thought, a tree is not what you think it is. It is something beyond the reach of thought, and to experience this 'something' is to perceive the mystery of life.

If our minds have become insensitive, what can we do? How can we be receptive to life and see the world with fresh eyes?

One thing we can do is to break our routine and move outside the circle in which we normally spend our lives. Even a simple change like travelling to work by a different route (or going by foot) can give us a slightly different perspective on the world. We can expose ourselves to different points of view through books, films and works of art, or by talking to people we don't usually meet. Missing several meals in a row or observing a 'buy nothing' day can remind us how a billion of our sisters and brothers spend every day of their lives.

But there's a simpler way to be aware – and that is to pause and open our eyes. Next time you are walking past a tree, look at it as if you had never seen a tree before. (If that doesn't work, try touching it.) When you are talking to a friend or business client, listen carefully to what they are saying and observe your own spoken and unspoken reactions. If you are preoccupied, notice that you are preoccupied. The very realisation that you have drifted into unawareness is itself the spark of awareness; you have already stepped outside the realm in which you were asleep.

There is a story about a sage who used to give a talk to his disciples each morning. One morning he laid out his mat and sat down, but just as he was about to start talking a bird started singing in a nearby tree. The sage waited quietly in deference to the bird, and it sang away merrily for some time. When the bird stopped the sage got up, rolled up his mat and said, 'That was the lesson for today'.

Opening our eyes

Helen Thomas

HOBART, AUSTRALIA

When I came back to Tasmania from overseas I realised something had changed inside me. I started to look at life differently; everything seemed clear and crisp. It was like wearing a very different pair of glasses. I could see and hear things I hadn't before. Sometimes I didn't know what was happening; it was almost overwhelming.

Once I was standing in Franklin Square, Hobart, waiting for the bus. People and pigeons were bustling about, and there were beautiful trees that have stood for hundreds of years. Nobody was looking at them! I had about twenty minutes before the bus came and my daughter Zoë was on my back. I looked up at the trees. I could see the leaves fluttering and the bright blue sky, and ... it was as if the trees were talking to me. It was all utterly magical.

There was a seagull nearby – for the first time, I really looked at a gull. I'd fed them and seen them flying around, but now that I really looked at one – it was just a perfect bird. Its white was pure white, its eyes were clear, its beak bright red; the colours were just amazing. Then it started to *fly* right in front of me, and I thought, 'Oh my *God*!'

It's like the world is magic – which it is if you really look at it. That's probably the way we're supposed to see it. Everything is amazing, and when you can see that, it makes you blissfully happy. At such moments it's as if the universe is talking to you, and you are finally listening. The opportunities to appreciate are endless but we lose that ability; we just don't see any more. We get busy and we forget to really look at things like the sky. I used to think, 'How can I have a spiritual experience in the middle of a city?' And I guess that's what they are – spiritual experiences.

I had a particularly powerful experience not long after I got married. I was at home by myself, feeling there were things in my life that I needed to forgive so I could move forward. I was looking in the mirror – I'd been putting something in my hair – and I started staring into my eyes. I saw sadness and hurt. Several years earlier I had been raped, and I hadn't been able to resolve the pain of that. I'd tried counselling, but it just hadn't worked, I wasn't moving forward. I stared deeper and deeper, and I realised I needed to go back to the place where I'd been hurt and forgive the person

who had raped me. I needed to go back to that place in order to love myself.

I imagined myself going back and forgiving that person; I also forgave someone else who had treated me badly. I'd had lots of hang-ups and felt so much anguish, and I just released it. I felt so light; from that moment on I started to see my eyes, my whole self, differently. My life is a huge mystery and I'm so excited about how I'm going to live now.

From that time on, all my relationships started to change. When you open yourself up to the universe, you start to see the beauty in people, and they can sense the change in you. Sometimes this has made things awkward because I'd be sitting with people I'd got along with before, and I'd realise we had little in common. I might say, 'My God, look at the sky!' and they'd answer, 'Oh yeah' and carry on talking. But I've also started to meet people who see the world differently; and when you meet people like that it makes up for anything lost.

One of the reasons I'd gone overseas was that I'd been unhappy at work – I'd been working as a political reporter for a newspaper. I used to think it was my problem because I had low self-esteem. But when I went back to work I realised, 'Hang on, it's not me, it's them! It wasn't me the whole time! I don't belong in this bureaucratic world of suits and egos!' I quit newspapers and continued journalism at a government agency. Within eighteen months I again heard my soul crying out for me to leave. If I'd stayed just for the money I wouldn't have been true to myself.

'When you open yourself up to the universe, you start to see the beauty in people, and they can sense the change in you.'

Two weeks after I quit my job my husband Gavin and I decided to have a baby. I started working from home as a freelance journalist, and I was able to spend the whole nine months in peaceful and beautiful surroundings. I think if every woman could do that, they'd find that pregnancy and birth are the most beautiful experiences in life.

Every day while I was pregnant I would go walking in the forest near where I live and talk with the 'Big Wise Tree'. I used to walk right past that tree without even noticing it, but one day I stopped and looked at it. It was massive, and although dead, there were mosses and mushrooms growing on it, and it was surrounded by ferns. All through my pregnancy that tree was my strength and a huge part of my growth. I talked to it, and I still do. People might think I'm silly talking to a tree, but it seems so natural. I feel that the tree is saying things to me, but then I wonder, 'Is it just me? Am I having a conversation with myself?' Either way, I'm clarifying things in my mind. After talking to the Big Wise Tree I feel like I've been on a long journey.

I was up there one dawn when I met Margie, a beautiful girl who had just moved into our neighbourhood. We stopped and chatted and I was telling her how I felt about the September 11 attacks, which had happened only a few days before. They had affected me deeply because I was about to bring a little baby into this world of terrorism. But then I realised that Zoë was hope, and that she could help to change the world.

After about twenty minutes we said goodbye. I walked on and she jogged off. She was already out of sight when I heard her voice call out, 'Helen!' It was like a voice from the sky. I'd never heard my name sound so beautiful. 'Helen!' she said, 'you really are a beautiful person!' I cried the whole way home. All through my life I'd thought I was not a very good person, not a beautiful person. I used to hate myself, and be cruel to myself. But to hear that, it was like an angel speaking.

Since becoming a mother, I've never been busier. I never underestimate how mysterious and beautiful it is to bring a baby into the world, but when I'm getting up five times during the night, that can be hard to remember! I'm starting to make more time now. It's partly a matter of motivation: I can sit here with Zoë and be boring, or we can go out and explore – because everything is new to her.

There was a beautiful moment when Zoë was little and I'd only recently started talking aloud to myself in the forest. Zoë was in front of me, facing out, and I was talking about my love for her and the amazing journey so far – the pregnancy and the birth. I went to turn her around because I thought she was about to fall asleep, and she had a little tear falling down. She wasn't crying; it was like she was really listening and understanding.

Gavin and I are now planning to work with a volunteer organisation somewhere in the developing world. We want to do something to help people who lack so many of the opportunities that Australians take for granted – although we're under no illusions that the 'developed' world has all the answers. We also want to give Zoë the chance to grow up in a place where community spirit doesn't take a back seat to consumerism. We know it's an unconventional course, and not all our friends will understand why we're taking it. You make your journey harder when you break away from the mainstream, and you need strength to deal with that. But if you didn't – if you just said, 'Well that's too hard, I'm going to go along with what they think' – you'd be an empty shell. You might get to the end of your life and think, 'Oh my God, I didn't listen to my heart, I didn't listen to my soul.'

Helen Thomas

7. Self-awareness

Self-awareness helps free us from the fear and ignorance that obstruct relationship.

Most of us experience the world through a prism that we call 'myself'. Our moods may fluctuate and our circumstances may change, but our sense of identity seldom varies. This apparently unchanging self is the central player in our lives. From the moment we get out of bed in the morning until we go to sleep at night it is our 'I' that is thinking and acting, scheming and judging, hoping and fearing, amusing itself and getting bored. It is 'I' that says 'my house', 'my job', 'my problems', 'my interests', 'my life'.

This sense of self is also one of the primary causes of friction between human beings. We spend the greater part of our lives immersed in our private pleasures and pains, and preoccupied with our own desires and anxieties; and the more we are thus immersed and preoccupied, the less capable we are of empathising with other people and seeing things from their point of view. My interests conflict with yours, and the battle begins.

Perhaps there are a few people who are entirely free of the sense of self as we normally experience it. The life stories and writings of some spiritual teachers — such as J. Krishnamurti and Ramana Maharshi — suggest that such freedom is possible. The rest of us are united (in a sense) by the very thing that separates us. Self-interest is self-interest the world over, although its mode of expression may vary. Greed is greed regardless of the pleasures we are greedy for. In this vital sense, to know ourselves is to know humanity because each of us represents humanity. By understanding the way greed operates in our own minds we can understand the greed of humanity. To the extent that we can free ourselves from greed, we will be helping humanity to be thus free.

Is it possible to be free of greed? Is it possible to live without self-interest, or to change our outlook so completely that our interests are no longer in conflict with the rest of the planet's? These are complex questions that deserve careful consideration. People have been striving for thousands of years to transcend the boundaries of the self. They have lived in monasteries, taken drugs, chanted, prayed and tortured themselves. If there were an easy path it would have been discovered long ago.

But selflessness is not some remote and unattainable goal. It can be as simple as one's love for a child or a spontaneous act of compassion. We can escape from ourselves in moments of joy or in the appreciation of something beautiful. We all know how it feels to empathise with another living creature. We have all had the experience of being moved by the happiness or sorrow of another human being.

Many of us realise that the world is in a terrible state and want to do something about it. We don't want to stand idly by while children starve and rainforests are destroyed. But if we are reasonably aware we can see that we are suffering from the very disease that is causing this chaos. If we are honest, we have to face the fact that we ourselves are aggressive and greedy. We may also be kind and considerate, but aggression and greed are woven into the fabric of our minds. So long as this remains true, the parts of our nature that are aggressive and greedy will poison our actions and sow seeds of violence in the world.

What can we do?

One thing we can do is to become more aware of our thoughts and actions in daily life. So long as we act without awareness, our actions will inevitably be influenced by our unconscious habits and prejudices. When we see our habits and prejudices for what they are, their influence declines and another factor comes into play – namely, the intelligence that comes with seeing. A simple exercise is to take a deep breath before responding to a question or a challenge, particularly in stressful situations. When we delay our habitual responses, we allow time for them to reveal themselves and for new insights to arise.

Being self-aware does not mean becoming self-obsessed or isolated in our private worlds. It simply means being aware in our daily lives – of the way we talk, of the way we respond to unexpected situations, of what makes us feel insecure or angry. As we journey into ourselves we can begin to explore the mystery of our own existence. Why do we live the way we do? What are our hidden motives and fears? Who is this 'I' whose demands and anxieties occupy such an enormous part of our lives? Am I the same 'I' who woke up this morning, who read the first chapter of this book? Am 'I' really separate from 'you' or from the breeze that comes through this window?

Faced as we are with so many problems – economic, political, environmental, social – can we afford the luxury of journeying inwardly into ourselves? Both inner and outer change are necessary, and awareness is the agent of change. Outer action is certainly needed to reform our social, economic and political systems; but there must also be a radical change in the way we think and the way we respond to the challenges of life.

This revolution in relationship must begin with the individual. The source of humanity's most urgent problems lies in human consciousness, and you and I are custodians of that consciousness. Through self-awareness we can begin to free ourselves from the ignorance, greed, deceit and fear that obstruct human relationship. Whatever changes we can bring about in our minds will influence our daily lives, and ultimately the world as a whole.

The transformation of suffering

Stephen Fulder

GALILEE, ISRAEL

Growing up in London as a child of German-Jewish refugees, I was keen to be free of the insecurity that I saw in my parents' generation. I found Judaism oppressive, and began exploring the whole Sixties phenomenon. At eighteen I went to California and found myself amidst the dynamic creativity of the psychedelic era. At the same time I kept my feet on the ground by pursuing studies in medical research.

To me, one of the important messages of the psychedelic movement was that mind is more important than matter; the reality we experience is not necessarily what is really going on. I first visited South Asia in 1967, hitchhiking from London to Lahore and back just for the hell of it. It seemed that 'mind over matter' existed in daily life in that part of the world; it wasn't just a theory. There was something about the inner freedom there that caught my imagination; it seemed a paradise after Europe's pretence and self-importance.

In 1975 I had the chance to go to India to teach biochemistry at Benares Hindu University in Varanasi. I taught for three months, and became increasingly fascinated by the spirituality of ordinary life. When my job ended I stayed on for another six months, living in a small room on the banks of the Ganges and worshipping with the *sadhus* (holy men). There were very few tourists in those days.

When I returned to England I did a post-doctorate, then taught at Chelsea College. I was interested in exploring different perspectives on medicine, particularly in relation to medicinal herbs, and I wrote a book called *The Root of Being*. I married an Israeli woman and together we began to look around for alternative communities where we could practise a creative and sustaining lifestyle. I was particularly influenced at that time by John Woods, who was interested in ecological philosophy and was part of the Sarvodaya movement.

In the early 1980s my wife and I joined several other families to start a community in the north of Israel. While I found the arrogance and militarism of Israeli society rather intimidating, I was fascinated by the spiritual dynamism of the place and by the sense that a great historical journal was being written there. Our community developed along Gandhian lines – we built our own houses,

grew our own food and lived simply without electricity. I learnt about building and farming as I went along, particularly from local Arab communities, and spent two years clearing stones from the fields. During this time I learnt about surrendering and letting go, as if something was being burnt from my personal history. I also devoted much of my energy to parenting my three daughters.

At the same time I found myself increasingly drawn to explore the spiritual sources of who I was and what I was doing. I read original Buddhist texts and invited Buddhist teachers to give courses in my house. It was the first time Buddhists had taught in Israel. We formed an organisation called The Insight Society ('Amutat Tovana' in Hebrew), and we now have around 2000 people on our mailing list in Israel and six or seven hundred coming to our annual meditation retreats.

Over time we began to help others, because spiritual practice makes you sensitive to others' needs while giving you the inner strength that makes it possible to help them. We decided to create some movement towards peace between Israelis and Palestinians – not out of any political orientation, but simply because the Palestinian issue was the dominant cause of suffering in the region. So we set up a program of two-day workshops called 'The transformation of suffering'. Our aim was to give Israelis and Palestinians opportunities to come together, acknowledge each other's suffering, and experience the hope and energy that come when suffering is released. Our approach was a logical outcome of Buddhist teachings, which say that if you acknowledge and hold your pain – instead of suppressing it or projecting it onto others – then that creates a movement to freedom.

Our main Palestinian partner, a woman called Rowdah Basir, was running a therapeutic kindergarten for traumatised Palestinian children. She had spent twelve years in Israeli jails, and had used that time to completely rid herself of hatred. She invited Palestinians from all levels of society – businesspeople, shopkeepers, farmers, professors – to our workshops. Once a month, fifteen Israelis would go into Palestinian territory to meet with an equal number of Palestinians. The journey itself was a profound challenge for the Israelis, who usually have no contact with Palestinians whatsoever. The warmth and hospitality they found touched their hearts.

'Once you receive the humanness of another you can no longer see him or her as an enemy.'

At the start of each workshop we tried to create a feeling of safety and security by playing simple games and ensuring that every word was translated. Then we would work in pairs and encourage people to talk about their lives. These exercises were a major release, especially for the Palestinians, who only ever saw Israeli soldiers and were desperate to tell their stories to ordinary Israelis. After each session we would reflect on what we had experienced, and it was at these times especially that we felt each other's humanness. That's where the real transformation takes place, because once you receive the humanness of another you can no longer see him or her as an enemy. Finally, we used the energy for change created by these sessions to generate ideas for new programs – for example, groups of Israelis going into Palestinian areas to teach computer skills or to replace olive trees the Israeli army had destroyed.

The workshops showed the Israelis that they didn't have to be afraid; that not every Palestinian wanted to throw them into the sea. They realised that the Palestinians were afraid, too, so that a chain reaction was going on; and that is a powerful understanding. For the Palestinians the greatest change was empowerment: they no longer felt quite as helpless or hopeless. The realisation that some Israelis understood what they were going through created a belief in humankind and allowed them to take a more philosophical view of the conflict. Teachers could go back to the children in their classes and help them make sense of what was happening around them.

We ran the workshops for about three years until the Palestinian Authority insisted that we conduct our activities as part of an official process that could demonstrate clear political outcomes. We could not continue on those terms, so we are currently focusing our efforts inside Israel. When the latest *intifada* (Palestinian uprising) erupted, a substantial proportion of Israelis went from a peace orientation to a defensive, almost war-like mentality: 'It's no use, nothing helps; you can say what you like about peace but when they're coming at you, you just have to fight.' This sense of helplessness and resignation is one of the problems we're trying to deal with – for example by organising peace walks and establishing a botanical garden (a joint Jewish–Arab project).

Our work is intended to deal with the sources of conflict, and because of this, we have no way of measuring its results. You might think, 'If I convince a hundred people, I've done a good job; if I convince only three, it's been a failure.' But that kind of thinking is misguided. No action is meaningless, and the integrity of even small actions makes waves that spread, changing hearts and minds in unknown ways.

Our workshops have had extraordinary results. One Israeli participant, Neta Golan, wanted to do more, so she began camping in Palestinian areas that were under threat from Israeli attack. She has been doing that ever since despite enormous personal risk. On one occasion she was beaten by Israeli soldiers and had her arm broken, but she came back with her arm in a sling only a day or two later. She has been in the newspapers repeatedly, and has probably saved dozens of lives.

At another workshop, two young men from Hamas came in off the street. They were aggressive, standing to one side and challenging the other Palestinians, 'Why are you talking to these people? They are killers', and 'This is only making the occupiers feel better.' We started to talk with them. Eventually they sat down and told their stories – stories of terrible deprivation and suffering – and the ice cracked. Some older Israeli women offered them help with their university studies, and so forth. At the end of the second day they said, 'We are very confused. We feel that it's wrong to be violent and we now see that there are other ways of doing things. As soon as we go back onto the streets we'll get drawn into the hatred and violence once more; but something has changed completely and we can never be the same again.'

Amazingly, those two men have kept in touch with us right through the latest *intifada*. Recently, one of them spoke on the phone to one of the older Israeli women, and he told her, 'I will always love you.'

Stephen Fulder

8. Global awareness

To live responsibly we need to understand the global consequences of our actions.

To live responsibly we need to be aware of the consequences of our actions, not only in our own neighbourhoods and countries but throughout the world. In social, political and environmental terms the world has become a very small place, with events and developments in one part of the world rapidly affecting the entire planet. A decision taken by London shareholders can cost the jobs of thousands of South Africans or wipe out a tract of Brazilian rainforest. A boycott of designer clothing in the United States can help to improve the working conditions of labourers in Bangladesh.

The last twenty years have seen vast changes in the global economic system, changes that have affected the lives of billions of people. Yet most of us who live in wealthy countries are only vaguely aware of these changes. How many of us realise, for example, that the economic crisis of 1997 cut real wages in Indonesia by up to 40 percent and more than doubled the number of Indonesians living in poverty? As a result of this disaster, up to three million Indonesian children are now malnourished and will grow up with health problems and disabilities. How many of us realise that recent changes in international trade regulations have led to the collapse of the Ghanaian rice industry? From being a net exporter of rice, Ghana is now forced to import it because subsidised US imports have undercut local producers. Dozens of other developing countries face similar problems. Per capita incomes declined in more than eighty countries during the 1990s. Moreover, pressure from organisations like the International Monetary Fund and the World Trade Organisation has fuelled escalating environmental destruction throughout much of the world.

Much of the responsibility for these developments lies with the governments of the world's wealthy nations. It is these governments that set the rules for global trade through institutions like the World Trade Organisation. It is these governments whose protectionist laws are costing developing countries more than $100 billion per year in lost trade opportunities, and whose aid budgets had dwindled to all-time lows by the beginning of this century.

If we vote for these governments we are also responsible. If we vote for politicians who support the existing global economic order, we share responsibility for the deterioration of the global environment and for the worsening economic situation of hundreds of millions of people. The fact that we may know little or nothing about global economics does not absolve us of responsibility. On the contrary, such ignorance is indefensible because it can have catastrophic consequences.

Television and newspapers bring us 'the news'. But the mainstream version of 'the news' presents a limited view of what is happening in the world. In the United States, for example, news bulletins rarely include stories from abroad unless the US is waging a war in some far-away country. Few Americans know about their government's role in training and funding death squads in Latin America during the last three decades of the twentieth century; or about America's support for the 1975 Indonesian invasion of East Timor, which resulted in the death of more than 200 000 East Timorese.

While Western politicians negotiate business deals with Chinese officials, few of us are more than dimly aware of the brutalities that the Chinese government is perpetrating in Tibet. One Tibetan monk, Palden Gyatso, was imprisoned in degrading conditions and repeatedly tortured for 33 years by the Chinese authorities. He was released in 1992 but hundreds of his compatriots remain in prison and thousands remain in exile. This didn't stop the United States from maintaining China's status as a 'Most Favoured Nation' trading partner during the 1990s, or prevent China's entry into the World Trade Organisation in 2001.

Our governments are implicated in genocide. Yet mainstream media pay little attention to what is happening in Tibet, or Chechnya, or Colombia, or the Kurdish sector of Turkey, and they largely ignore the terrible human cost of globalisation in the developing world.

Yet the media can play a vital role in precipitating positive change. In the mid 1990s, the *Virgin Islands Daily News* (whose circulation was then 17 500) ran a ten-part story exposing widespread crime and corruption in the US Virgin Islands. The story, which won a Pulitzer Prize (journalism's highest award in the US), resulted in the dismissal of several top Virgin Islands officials and a substantial drop in the local crime rate. International media exposure of the injustices of the pre-1994 South African government helped to bring down the apartheid regime. When demonstrators take to the streets they do so partly with the aim of attracting publicity, thereby putting pressure on politicians and corporate decision-makers.

We don't need to be passive consumers of 'the news'. A wide variety of information channels exists including 'alternative' radio stations, the Internet and magazines published

by social-justice oriented nongovernment organisations. Books and articles by commentators such as Noam Chomsky and John Pilger have exposed the ugly realities beneath the gloss of political and corporate propaganda. The 'letters to the editor' and 'opinion' pages of newspapers and magazines can alert readers to issues that would otherwise receive little or no attention.

We can start our own newspapers or magazines. If you think this sounds impractical you should talk to Jason Crowe, an American who in 1996 started a 'kids for kids' newspaper called *The Informer* when he was just nine years old. The newspaper is now distributed in sixteen countries, and Jason's work as a peace activist has attracted the support of Joan Baez, Pete Seeger, Bono and other celebrities. We can attend public meetings and listen to talks by visiting speakers. If we have the resources we can travel to other parts of the world and see what is happening with our own eyes.

If you become better informed about what's happening in the world, what difference will it make? You might change your voting habits. You might lobby politicians to support progressive foreign policies. You might think twice about buying a pair of shoes, knowing that they have been manufactured by what is effectively slave labour. You might think twice about *everything* you buy, knowing that the environmental destruction and the economic injustices that are necessary to sustain the developed world's excessive consumption are creating misery for millions of people and eroding the security of future generations.

The realisation that you are a citizen of a finite and interconnected world could have far-reaching consequences for the way you think and live.

The wider world

Joliz Cedeño

NEW YORK CITY, USA

I was born in Manhattan but I grew up in the South Bronx, Puerto Rico and Florida. In Puerto Rico I lived in a tiny neighbourhood surrounded by other members of my family. Our house was close to several bars; when I went to buy lollypops I'd be standing there at the counter beside old men drinking alcohol. My upbringing was fairly strict and traditional – being a girl, I had to learn how to cook and clean. But my mother always emphasised that I could do anything and did not have to limit myself on account of my gender.

When I was fourteen my family moved back to the South Bronx, and life there was very different. Although most of the people in our area were Puerto Rican, they were more money-oriented than people in Puerto Rico were, and the differences between rich and poor were clearer. Taking the train from downtown to uptown you could see where the people with money lived, and it was obvious that most of the landfills, incinerators and polluting factories were in the lower income neighbourhoods. This is really a form of racism because the people who live in these neighbourhoods are mostly from ethnic minorities.

My mother sent me to a progressive high school on the Upper West Side, which was lucky for me because our local high school in the South Bronx was the most violent in New York City. The Beacon School was community-oriented in the sense that every teacher knew who you were and listened to what you had to say – unlike my previous schools, where you were just another kid among hundreds. Learning at the Beacon School focuses on understanding rather than cramming for exams, and assessment is based mainly on essays and one-to-one discussions with teachers.

During my early school years I had learnt very little about what was happening in the wider world. Even in Puerto Rico we were taught American history rather than the history of Puerto Rico. In Florida I learnt to say 'Hello' and 'Good morning' in other languages, and we talked about the Eiffel Tower, but that was about it. One of my brothers was in the army, and when he told me he'd been to Kosovo I had no idea where that was. This started to change at Beacon High, where students are required to do fifty hours of community service as part of the curriculum. One of my

options was to help produce a radio program, and I thought that sounded cool: I imagined I'd be sitting there talking about the songs I'd picked out. But it turned out to be very different.

The radio program had three million listeners and was run by Global Kids, a New York-based organisation that is fostering multiculturalism, global responsibility and leadership skills among urban youth. The first show we produced was on AIDS in the US and Africa, and I was one of the presenters. Other programs were on issues like police brutality, environmental racism and sexuality. I also became involved in workshops and forums that addressed issues ranging from child soldiers and sweatshops to genetically modified food and US–Cuba relations. I had to do my own research, and the more I found out about these things the more I wanted to learn. I started to realise that there is another world outside the US and that so much of what we do here affects people in other parts of the world.

The Global Kids workshops, which were usually attended by about thirty young people, involved experiential activities such as role-playing or watching a video and then debating the issues that it raised. These sessions were invaluable because they taught us how to listen to other points of view and how to debate without attacking people on a personal level. Some of the kids who came to these workshops felt that because we were talking about other parts of the world, the issues didn't matter for us. But the whole point is to realise that these issues do matter, even if they don't affect us directly.

At the end of my first year with Global Kids I volunteered as one of the MCs for the organisation's annual conference, and the following year I facilitated one of the conference workshops by myself. That was particularly challenging because the topic was homophobia and some of the students who attended it had very narrow views on the subject. Even though I'm heterosexual myself, I found it painful to hear some of what was said – outright attacks on people just because they were different. By the end of the workshop I felt drained, but I think some of the participants realised that their views were a form of oppression, and that being from an oppressed minority doesn't mean you can't be an oppressor yourself.

'Being from an oppressed minority doesn't mean you can't be an oppressor yourself.'

In 2001 I went to Croatia with a fellow Global Kids student called DeShawn Cook and two supervisors. Global Kids has been organising visits to Croatia for several years to foster dialogue between young people with different ethnic backgrounds. Before we went we studied the history of the ethnic conflicts in the region, and DeShawn and I had to raise part of the funding for our trip. It was my first trip outside the US (except to Puerto Rico) and it was an intense experience in many ways. We spent the first week in Zagreb, where we attended a summer university with students from all over Europe. DeShawn and I were the most 'colourful' people there and we encountered a lot of racial hostility – especially DeShawn, who is Panamanian and has much darker skin than me.

From Zagreb we went to Knin, which had been one of the first towns in Croatia to be overrun by the 1991–95 war. As we drove through the town we saw blown-up houses and bullet-riddled walls. We also saw a lot of swastikas, because during World War II many Croatians had adopted Hitler's ideas. We were told harrowing stories about how people had cleared mines by sending out their sheep or even tried to clear them themselves. There was a pervasive sense of hopelessness among the people of Knin because out of a population of 16 000, fewer than 1500 had jobs.

When we arrived at the youth centre in Knin we were greeted like celebrities, but our stay there was very difficult. Most of the youths there were male, many of them were much older than me and some of them had actually fought in the war. I found it intimidating being the only female facilitator. During one of our sessions – an 'ice-breaking' activity in which each person was asked to perform an activity that represented who they were – one of the young men did a 'Heil Hitler' salute. It took them a while to open up to us, so I told them about my experiences back home and how, even though I'd never been through a war, I knew what it was like to hear gunshots outside my window. That's the reality in the South Bronx. They were amazed because they thought everything was perfect in America, and when they realised that we could empathise with them, they began to tell us about their own lives.

We returned to New York on September 9, 2001, two days before the World Trade Center attacks. The Global Kids office is in downtown Manhattan, and two of our staff actually saw the planes hit the towers. After the attacks Global Kids organised workshops to discuss the underlying issues that led to the attacks and the role that the US has played in the Middle East in recent decades. We also talked about prejudice against Muslims – a particularly relevant topic for us because many of our members are Muslim and a lot of them have experienced abuse, particularly since September 11.

I'm now studying at college but I still regularly take part in Global Kids activities. One of the programs that I'm involved in here is called the 'Tunnel of Oppression', which has been organised by a group called the Centre for Peace and Social Justice. The tunnel has been set up in a hall in the student union building. As people walk through it they see a succession of displays and short performances that represent every type of oppression you can imagine – from gay bashing to homelessness to rape to the mistreatment of animals. At the end of it they take part in a forum where they share what they have seen and felt. Hundreds of people have been through the tunnel and many of them say that they have been deeply moved by the experience.

I'm very concerned about where our country is heading. It scares me a lot that our president can now do what he likes with the military and exert so much power over the rest of the world. But I'm convinced that ordinary citizens can make a difference. Young people especially need to think for themselves and understand their rights and freedoms, because as they grow older they're the ones who are going to be voting and making decisions. We need to understand what's happening in our communities and in the world, because it's up to us to make the change.

Joliz Cedeño

Principles

of

Action

9. Respect

To respect is to acknowledge the sacred in the Earth and in all living things.

To act responsibly is to act with respect – for our fellow human beings, for other living creatures, for the Earth, for life and for ourselves. When we have respect we consider the needs of others and consequently limit our own demands. When we lack respect we trample on others, mistreat our fellow creatures and mutilate the Earth – as many of us are doing now.

We are all more or less familiar with the outward expressions of respect. If I respect you I won't try to shout you down or cut across what you are trying to say. If I respect the natural world I won't break a branch off a tree unnecessarily or use up fossil fuels as if doing so were my God-given right. But what is my motive for being respectful? What is the underlying source of respect?

There is something deeply mysterious about respect, something that cannot be rationalised or explained away. Why should I respect a tree, a bird or another human being? Why should I refrain from killing things unless I really need to kill them? I may go through the motions of respect because I want to appear respectable; but if I don't *feel* respect, my outer actions will have no integrity and will ultimately lack true respect. The feeling of respect cannot be calculated or contrived; it has to come from the heart.

Respect comes naturally when we recognise the inherent value of things. The members of many indigenous communities treat animals and plants with reverence, doing no more harm than is necessary to sustain their basic needs. In the so-called developed world we kill animals on conveyor belts and mow down trees as if they were weeds. The failure of the agricultural industry to respect the fact that cows are herbivorous was largely responsible for the scourge of BSE (commonly known as 'mad cow disease') and its human variant vCJD (variant Creutzfeldt-Jakob disease), which by 2003 had killed more than 120 people and may continue to kill people for decades to come.

So it is important that children be encouraged to understand and feel respect from a tender age, before they become excessively cynical or stupefied by consumerism. They should be encouraged to look at the sky and the trees, to feel the life pulsing in a leaf and the vitality of a bird in flight. They should be encouraged to respect themselves — and the best way to help them in this is for the adult to respect the child, because to feel respected is to experience one's own worth through someone else's eyes.

It is especially important to have self-respect — which is not to suggest that we should become vain or give undue importance to our personal gratification. Respecting ourselves means recognising our potential for integrity and our capacity to make a positive contribution to the world.

When we lack self-respect we tend to fall into various forms of delinquency. It could be said that contemporary Western society as a whole is delinquent because in many respects we are living negligently, preoccupied with trivial pleasures. If we respected ourselves we would not waste our lives doing meaningless work to purchase amusements we don't really want. If we had self-respect we would think for ourselves and not allow our brains to be programmed by advertising agencies and political spin-doctors.

Given sufficient care and attention, delinquency can be rectified. In many Western countries, programs have been established to help at-risk youth find the self-respect they need to live with passion and dignity. Most of these programs focus on developing self-reliance and non-aggressive social skills in challenging settings such as theatre groups, tall ships, craft workshops and wilderness areas. One such program, YARD (Youth At Risk Dancing), gives inner-city male teenagers in Cleveland, Ohio the opportunity to learn professional skills while expressing themes from their lives through dance. Almost all the teenagers who graduate from the program complete high school, and most go on to higher education or to join professional dance companies.

How are we to respect people whose actions seem to us contemptible, or at best unwise? The answer lies partly in recognising that there is goodness in almost everyone, and that many people are struggling with far greater difficulties than we are. We all do contemptible things at times, and we often condemn in others the insecurities or insensitivity that we fail to recognise in ourselves. If we can put aside our judgements of others, we may find ourselves surprised by their courage or humbled by their generosity. When we treat other people with respect, they almost always respond in kind.

When there is respect there is honour. 'Honour' is a powerful word, but it has fallen even further into disuse than 'respect'. It carries a sense of dignity, humility and reverence. To respect a tree is to honour it for its life, its history, its beauty, its mystery. To respect another human being is to honour that person regardless of gender, age, race, religion, sexual orientation or cultural background; it means not exploiting that person or indulging in activities that contribute to his or her exploitation. Ultimately, to respect is

to recognise that all living things are manifestations of the intelligence of the universe –
an intelligence vastly beyond the reach of thought or imagination.

There is a sequel to that story about when I was a track-worker. On one occasion a
colleague and I were in an area where good timber was scarce, and we found a tree that
would have supplied all the timber we needed for several days. It was a magnificent tree
that seemed to hold sway over all the forest around it. As we were sizing it up, we began
to notice birds of many different species; the longer we stood there, the more its branches
seemed to fill with birds. It was as if all those birds were flocking to the tree and saying,
'Don't take this one! This is the Lord of the Forest!' To fell that tree would have been
sacrilege. So we paid our respects and left it in peace.

To respect is to acknowledge the sacred in the Earth and in all living things.

Seeds of renewal

Cathrine Sneed

SAN FRANCISCO, USA

I grew up wanting to become a criminal lawyer because I wanted to be able to help my brothers if they ever got into trouble as victims of racism. Racism permeates every aspect of our culture, although as a child you experience it differently. At the Catholic high school I attended, the African-American children were encouraged to take technical classes rather than college prep classes. I remember one of the nuns saying to me, 'Why are you bothering to take college prep? You people don't go to college.' But fortunately there were also nuns who encouraged me to go to college and law school.

One of my professors at the college where I studied law, Michael Hennessey, ran a legal services program for prisoners. Michael was different from the other lawyers I'd met in that he cared about the prisoners and understood that they needed the kind of help that people with money get routinely. His outlook impressed me deeply, and it was largely thanks to him that I changed from wanting to be a hotshot lawyer to wanting to help people stay out of jail. Most of the people in our county jail were petty criminals who were in on alcohol and drug-related offences. Basically, most of them were in jail because they were poor.

When Michael became Sheriff of San Francisco County he offered me a job as a prison counsellor with the Sheriff's Department. I was 24 and had two children. I worked mainly with women prisoners and I did what I could for them, but I wasn't making much difference. It wasn't enough to find a prisoner a new set of clothes or to find out where the police had taken a mother's children when she was jailed for prostitution. Many of these people had limited reading skills and no work experience. If they applied for a job, one of the first questions they'd be asked was, 'Have you ever been arrested?' and if they said 'Yes' they wouldn't be hired. The rejection reinforced their belief that they had no place in society, and they'd go back to selling drugs or selling themselves to survive. And then of course they'd come back to jail. That was very hard on me, physically and emotionally, because I identified with those people as men and women of colour.

I'd been working with these people for several years when I developed a serious kidney disease. After a year of going in and out of hospital my doctor said, 'It doesn't look good. You're not responding to drugs. You can either stay here in the hospital and die, or you can go home and die.' On the day he told me that news, a friend gave me a copy of John Steinbeck's *The Grapes of Wrath*. I found a powerful message in it: that when people feel a connection with the land, they have a reason to live and they can find their way through any difficulty. I felt that if we could just get the prisoners outside and onto the land, we would at least have a chance.

That's when I had the idea of starting an organic garden at San Francisco jail, which stands on what used to be a 145-acre farm. Michael Hennessey supported the idea, and as we started clearing the site and planting seeds, the prisoners began to work together and to feel that they were making a difference. They had found an activity that meant something to them. Witnessing the cycle of growth and renewal allowed them to see their own potential for growth and change. It also helped me to go into remission, which is where I am still.

But the prison garden wasn't enough to keep these people out of jail. As soon as they were released they would go back to the hotel rooms or housing projects no-one should live in, back to the lives they were living before. Some prisoners were glad to come back to jail because the gardening experience meant more to them than anything outside.

We needed to develop projects that released prisoners could participate in. We began in the early 1990s with a volunteer tree-planting project, and soon the city council started employing former prisoners to plant trees. In the past ten years they've planted over 10 000 trees, mostly in poor neighbourhoods. Now the people in those neighbourhoods see trees where there used to be bare sidewalks and garbage. And they see people who used to sell drugs on the corner trying their darnedest to care for these trees.

In 1992 we developed the project further by starting an organic garden on a half-acre plot in the Bayview district of San Francisco. At any one time the garden has employed as many as 125 former prisoners, many of whom go on to work as gardeners or maintenance workers for the city council. We require our employees to work a minimum of 40 hours a week and to study for a high school diploma if they don't have one. We pay them $11 an hour, enough to support their families. They also receive medical and dental benefits.

We donate most of our produce to working families and retired seniors who are struggling to make ends meet. More than 22 percent of African-Americans and Latinos in this city go hungry, and the figure is increasing. Last year we donated over 10 000 pounds (4500 kilos) of vegetables including broccoli, Swiss chard, potatoes, cauliflower, lettuces and squashes. We work with community centres to produce fliers with information about nutrition, because many people do not know the dietary importance of vegetables or even how to cook them. One of our community organisations has also begun a cooking class, for which we supply the vegetables.

'When we lack the faith that these people can change we're expressing a lack of faith in our own humanity.'

Most of our funding comes from the local government. The Police Department helps us distribute the food, and it's often the first time the officers have had a positive interaction with their neighbourhoods. In 2002 we also began a community-supported agriculture program to support our work. It gives local customers the opportunity to buy a share of each harvest, which we deliver to their homes. We sell some food and flowers to local restaurants, we have a stall at the Ferry Plaza Farmers' Market, and every Halloween we donate over 8000 pumpkins to schools in poor neighbourhoods.

Many of our employees are single parents and we encourage them to bring their children to the Bayview garden. In summer we also have children's groups at the prison garden, which is near San Francisco airport. It is quite wild out there – we see bobcats, coyotes, even mountain lions. Most of the children have had minimal contact with the natural world, and they are amazed when they see lizards or hear coyotes barking. We also have a program for single mothers who are getting paid to set up and maintain gardens at schools in a number of poor neighbourhoods. So now, when the kids go to school they see flowers instead of graffiti and weeds.

Since we began the Garden Project in 1984 more than 10 000 prisoners have been involved and it has had a profound effect on many of them. By caring for plants and watching them grow they learn the true nature of this life: growth, renewal, and perseverance. By acquiring skills and earning enough to support their families they find that they have a purpose in life. Some of the program participants do voluntary work for people they used to steal from, and this helps to restore their self-respect. Three-quarters of our employees do not return to jail.

I recently saw one of our former employees weeding the freeway. He was limping badly because before he joined our program he'd been addicted to drugs and he'd been shot nine times and left for dead. When I asked him how he was doing he said, 'For the first time I can buy my daughters their school clothes, and it feels wonderful. I don't have to lie to them, I don't have to hide from them, I don't have to worry that I'm in jail. It makes me feel like I'm a real father.' One of the women in our program had been on the streets since she was thirteen and she'd had all five of her children taken from her because they were born addicted to drugs. Now she has all her children back and one of them just graduated from high school.

For years we've had this huge wave of hysteria in the US about people who use drugs. We've spent billions trying to keep them out of our face: there are more than two million people in America's prisons and the current trend is to say we need more prisons and harsher sentencing. This means we're giving up on our fellow human beings; and when we lack the faith that these people can change we're expressing a lack of faith in our own humanity. One in three young African-American men is either in prison or on parole, so even the youngest get the message that they are more likely to end up in jail than in college. In California we spend more on prisons than we do on schools. That is criminal.

As a mother this concerns me deeply, and when I started this program I had my children in mind big time. All these people were coming out of jail and they were going to be on the bus with my kids. What could I do to help them so that they wouldn't hurt my children? The people who join our program are in need of restoration; they're working to restore themselves, their families, their neighbourhoods and communities. In the Garden Project we're not just growing plants – we're growing people.

Cathrine Sneed

10. Simplicity

Mohandas Gandhi once said, 'Our world has enough for each person's need, but not for his greed'. Canadian researchers have estimated that if all the people now living in the world were to enjoy the current wealth of North Americans, we would need at least two additional Planet Earths. North Americans and the citizens of other wealthy nations are able to live as they do because the world's wealth is neither used sustainably nor distributed equitably. The world's richest 50 million people are collectively as wealthy as the poorest 2.7 billion people. Australia consumes 80 percent as much oil as Indonesia, which has twelve times Australia's population.

The world's environmental problems are also disproportionately caused by the rich nations. The United States, with less than 5 percent of the world's population, produces a quarter of the world's greenhouse gases. The richest one-fifth of the world's population consume four-fifths of the planet's resources — which means they are responsible for most of the logging, mining, damming, dumping and bulldozing.

Billions of the world's people lack the basic necessities of dignified living. The Western world could, if it wished, go a long way towards providing those necessities. A 1998 United Nations report estimated that basic education, health care, food, safe water and sanitation could be provided to everyone who now lacks these things for around $28 billion per year – less than Europeans and Americans spend on pet food and cosmetics. The abolition of subsidies that allow Western corporations to undercut producers in the Third World could generate income and employment for millions of people in developing countries. The cancellation of Third World debt would ease the financial burden on the world's poorest countries, some of which (for example Zambia and Tanzania) have been paying more on debt servicing than on health or education.

It is only natural that people living in shantytowns or impoverished villages should want a better deal. But those of us who live in the developed world are not satisfied either. We have created an economic system geared to endless growth – growth in the sense of ever-increasing production and consumption. Without growth, we are told, progress would grind to a halt and our children would be left without a future. But the long-term prospects for growth do not look encouraging, as anyone with a hand-held calculator can demonstrate. A 'healthy' growth rate of 3 percent per annum equates to a doubling of economic activity every 24 years and a hundred-fold increase every 156 years. Imagine a hundred-fold increase in energy consumption or a hundred times more output of garbage. Perpetual growth on a finite planet simply doesn't compute.

Even our current levels of consumption are unlikely to be sustainable for very much longer. We might like to think that our way of life is, as former US president George Bush Snr famously expressed it, 'not up for negotiation'. But if the world experiences massive environmental and associated economic collapse, precipitating suffering and conflict on an unprecedented scale, then our stock market portfolios will be of little use to us and our home entertainment system will be small consolation.

The economic growth of the past 50 years has undoubtedly brought benefits. But has it made us happier? Per capita wealth in industrialised countries has more than doubled since 1960, yet surveys suggest that people in these countries are not much happier than they were 40 years ago. A greater gain in community wellbeing might have been achieved by redirecting 5 percent of each country's military spending to improving public transport or to job-creation schemes. Job satisfaction in Britain and America has not risen since the 1970s, and the suicide rate for men in most Western countries has increased over the last twenty years. A survey conducted in 1989 found that 75 percent of working Americans between the ages of 25 and 49 wanted to see their country 'return to a simpler lifestyle, with less emphasis on material success'.

If getting richer isn't making us happier, why do we want more? Is it because advertisements keep persuading us to want more? Are we are trying to compensate for the insufficiency of our daily lives? Could it be that we are literally addicted to consumption?

It's nice to buy a shiny new car or a beautiful piece of furniture. But when the pleasure of acquisition wears off, the feeling of insufficiency returns — a feeling that no amount of shopping can alleviate. And advertisements exploit this feeling. I once heard a radio advertisement that exhorted the listener to 'take control of your destiny. Power to the people ... ' the lyrics ran, ' ... not secondhand or imaginary'. The advertisement was for a range of sportswear. See how cunning the ad people are: in an age of video surveillance and rising sea levels, they bait the hook with high-sounding rhetoric about taking control of our destiny. But all they are really offering — at a price — is the 'freedom' to make a fashion statement.

Consumerism functions by keeping us in a state of chronic dissatisfaction. If we were satisfied we would want very little and we would not be taken in by advertisements. We are junkies, consuming things that soon becomes junk (if they are not junk already!) — and the advertising industry is the world's biggest pusher.

One of the greatest challenges that now faces us in the West is finding ways to live richly and happily while curbing our material consumption. Much of the groundwork has already been done. Around the world, thousands of people are already living in eco-villages and similar communities established with the specific aim of creating sustainable living environments. In Nottinghamshire, England, for example, a recently opened housing project features five houses that generate their own wind-powered electricity, collect their own water and recycle human waste using a pollution-free reed bed system. Co-housing projects give people the option of owning their own houses while sharing facilities such as workshops, guest rooms and children's play areas.

Increasing numbers of people are subscribing to community-supported agriculture, a scheme in which groups of people pay money in advance to local farmers to cultivate the produce they want. Under this scheme the risks and benefits of farming are shared, costs are not inflated by long-distance transportation or unnecessary wholesaling, the carbon emissions associated with transportation are reduced – and subscribers receive a box of fresh vegetables every week.

Many people have turned away from excessively materialistic lifestyles, realising that there is more to life than stock options and frequent-flyer accounts. David Tagliani used to live what some might consider the ultimate success story: he had a million-dollar job as senior manager of Microsoft's worldwide operations. But he had also reached what he describes as 'a level of burnout that I never thought possible'. After quitting his job and backpacking around the world for two years, David started teaching computer skills at an orphanage in Russia. He now runs an Internet café in Moscow, employing orphaned youngsters who might otherwise be headed for lives of crime or prostitution.

Making the transition to a sustainable economy doesn't necessarily mean we can't have economic growth. But we will have to redefine what we mean by growth, and indeed redefine what we mean by wealth. The traditional indicator of a nation's wealth, namely its gross national product (GNP), is primarily a measure of financial transactions; it ignores quality-of-life factors such as job security, air quality and the depletion of non-renewable resources. Economists are now beginning to develop measures of wealth that take these factors into account – and by these measures we may be able to enjoy 'growth' indefinitely.

In Japan, where the economy has been sluggish for several years, local governments are introducing their own currencies to boost employment and revive a sense of community spirit. In the city of Chiba, near Tokyo, people are literally working for 'peanuts' – as the local currency is whimsically called. One of the rules of the 'peanut' system is that whenever people conduct a transaction they have to shake hands and shout (in Spanish) 'Amigo!' Elsewhere in Japan, people are working for currencies called 'dan dan' ('thank-you's) or 'rabu' ('love').

But when we spend regular currency we can purchase from businesses that deal fairly with their suppliers, particularly suppliers in developing countries. In the year 2000 the town of Garstang in Lancashire, England (pop. 5000) proclaimed itself as the world's first 'fair-trade town'. All of Garstang's schools and churches and 90 percent of its traders pledged to sell or use fair-trade products. Even at London's Clapham Junction railway station – a place I used to think of as the epitome of urban alienation – there is now a kiosk with a large sign that says 'Ethically sourced organic coffee'. It's only a small step, but the day I saw that sign I felt that there was hope for the world.

Sufficiency

Christian Leppert

BLACK FOREST, GERMANY

When I left university I wanted to find out what it means to live ecologically and sustainably, not just in theory or on weekends but as a 365-day-a-year experience. My background is in science but I was not interested in pursuing an academic career because basically we know what is going on. We know why the trees and forests are dying; we know how global warming works. What we don't know is how to switch to a sustainable lifestyle without generating psychological pollution – that is, conflict between how we live and how we think we *should* be living. Can we live responsibly and carefully without creating this conflict? That is the question I have been exploring for the past twenty years.

In 1980 I visited a so-called 'integral urban house' in California where young people were proving that you could live sustainably in a city. They had a garden, a windmill, solar power, and they cooked their own bread in a solar oven. I was completely thrilled, and I immediately knew that I wanted to do something similar. At that time many people in Germany were interested in trying to live sustainably. But land was (and is) very expensive here, so a lot of these people went to countries like Ireland, Canada and Australia, where land could be bought cheaply. I felt that if it is possible to live sustainably then it ought to be possible to do so in one's own country. When my wife Monika and I were looking for a house we had less than 2000 marks – scarcely enough to buy a garden shed. We found a beautiful property called 'Haus Sonne' ('Sun House') in the Black Forest which was for sale for 680 000 marks. The banks told us it was out of the question to finance such a project, but we borrowed money from friends and bought it anyway. For the past twenty years we've been running Haus Sonne as a guesthouse and educational centre with a focus on ecological and sustainable living.

Our first major project was building solar energy systems for cooking, heating and generating electricity. This meant we could reduce our fossil fuel consumption and we didn't have to buy electricity generated from nuclear power. Ten years ago we converted from gas to firewood, which I cut (with permission!) in the surrounding woodlands. I still use petrol for the chainsaw and diesel

for our 42-year-old tractor, but we no longer need fossil energy for cooking or heating. Our petrol station will soon offer bio-diesel and I am sure our old tractor will run just as well on it.

In 1990 Monika and I separated, Monika returning to a career in architecture specialising in ecological design. At Haus Sonne my new partner Eva and I began working with other ecological aspects of our lives such as food, clothing, sustainable building and our daily patterns of consumption. We always try to find out where all our purchases come from, and to support ethically and environmentally responsible manufacturers. A T-shirt from India is cheap because nobody cares about the low-paid workers – not to mention the ecological costs of long-distance transportation.

Our preference is to produce things ourselves instead of spending our lives earning money to buy things from other people. Food production is not so easy at an altitude of 1000 metres, which in this part of Germany is close to the limit of where you can live from your land. But local people with farm gardens lived here sustainably for centuries until mass production made it easier for them to buy their food in shops. We started with apple trees and a wide variety of berries, and I've just begun a large vegetable garden and a greenhouse. I've had to put in a snail fence because a lot of bugs that weren't here ten years ago have started moving into the mountains. We don't need extra proof of global warming – we can see it at our front door.

In our daily lives almost everything we do – whether it is driving a car, going to the cinema, buying clothes or paying a phone bill – causes some carbon dioxide to be released into the atmosphere. In the early 1990s Greenpeace and several other organisations circulated a questionnaire that allowed people to calculate how much carbon dioxide they were personally responsible for. If we don't want to accelerate global warming, each of us should release no more than one tonne of carbon dioxide per year. People in Western countries are generating many times that amount. Eva and I calculated our own carbon dioxide output and found that the use of our car was the worst thing in our carbon balance, even though we were not doing much travelling. So we sold our car and for the past ten years we've done most of our travelling on foot or by bicycle.

'To a large extent, living sustainably is about questioning what you really need.'

For us, a round trip to one of the larger cities (Basel or Freiburg) takes at least five hours by bicycle and involves an 800-metre climb on the return journey. A trip to the bank requires a two-and-a-half-hour hike. We use public transport for longer distances. We don't think of this as giving something up, but as gaining a better quality of life. Living sustainably means living at a slower pace, and in the process you become more sensitive. When you ride a bike or walk, you have time to appreciate the beauty of the landscape. You also become aware of the brutality of roads and cars and you don't want to be part of that.

Most of us don't see the connection between the way we are living and the disasters that are happening around the world. When you drive a car you ignore the exhaust because it's out behind the car and its effects are not immediate. If you put the exhaust inside the car the situation would change immediately! The same is true when you travel by plane. I like to use the example of chocolate: if eating chocolate made our teeth fall out immediately we'd stop eating it immediately, but we don't stop because our teeth might take twenty years or more to decay and it's easy to ignore long-term effects.

Sustainable living often comes down to simple, practical things. You might be in your workshop and discover that you need some nails. Normally you think you need them right now, so you get in your car and drive to the nearest store. If you took time to think about the situation you might work out a way to do the job without nails, or decide that you can get on with another job until you really need to go to the store. If you're building a house you might put in an ecological heating system or decide that by wearing a sweater you can stand an extra two degrees of cold. The more you experiment, the more you discover low-tech solutions – or, better still, no-tech solutions!

In 1998 we had the opportunity to build an extension to Haus Sonne; Monika was our architect. We built the extension with brick, local timber and mineral-plaster, using no paint or plastic and only low-tech plumbing and wiring. It has wooden floors, a grass roof (overhanging to protect our larch windows and doors), wood heating and solar power, and we insulated it with two and a half tonnes of German sheep wool. We did everything we could ourselves, and it was a great experience. The new building has a very special atmosphere and is beautiful to live in.

People come to Haus Sonne and share in our experiments. Many come for their holidays, to enjoy the beauty of the mountains, to relax in a non-smoking and non-alcohol environment and to treat themselves to our delicious, organically grown food. We also offer seminars and courses, and sometimes we have groups of young people stay for a couple of weeks or longer.

To a large extent, living sustainably is about questioning what you really need. If you are convinced you need a lot of things, then you need a lot of money to buy them. So then you need to work very hard, you don't have much free time, and when you get your holiday you fly to the other side of the world to make sure that you have sun in the few weeks that you have to recover! When you buy fewer things you need less money, and if you work less each day then every day you have free time in which to relax, recover and be creative.

When you are living a mainstream life it's easy to think that change is impossible and that there's no way out. But you don't have to get out of it completely; you can transform it, you can look at things differently. Then you begin to discover an incredible freedom. Then most of the things that belong to the capitalist world have little meaning, so you don't have to work to pay for them and you can lead a better life. When people tell me they want to live differently, I tell them 'Do it! Go for it! It is possible!'

Christian Leppert

II. Love

When we feel a sense of communion with the universe, we can act from love.

If you want to make a positive contribution to the world, one of the best ways to go about it is to find out what you love to do and then do it with all your heart and soul. This statement may surprise you because we tend to think that making a contribution involves some kind of personal sacrifice. It may; but that doesn't mean we have to sacrifice our hearts. It is when we act from greed or fear that we sacrifice our hearts.

Most of us know people who have the good fortune to spend their lives doing something they love. They might be scientists, or artists, or round-the-world sailors; or they might live unexceptional lives but love what they do anyway. But so many of us just muddle along without any real passion or sense of purpose, relieving the tedium of our lives by plugging into the entertainment grid.

If we live this way, we either give up hope or we live in the hope of achieving some kind of future goal such as buying a better house, winning the lottery or just having a few beers at the end of the day. There is nothing wrong with having goals, but if we become too goal-oriented we can spend most of our lives trying to get somewhere and very little time appreciating where we actually are. We can also become excessively competitive, shunning consideration and kindness in the stampede to 'get ahead'. In parts of

East Asia, children as young as two are being forced to sit for exams and six-month-old babies are being sat in front of instructional videos for up to seven hours a day. In their anxiety to see them succeed, the parents and teachers of these children are denying them the freedom of childhood.

You might say that if we all did what we loved, society wouldn't be able to function. But society isn't functioning now — unless its function is to suck the lifeblood out of the Earth and spit it out in ever-expanding heaps of unserviceable appliances. You might say that not everyone has the opportunity to do what they love. That is certainly true for those living in poverty; but need it be true for those of us who are not? When you really love something you find a way to do it.

I know a man, Tony Moscal, who was inspired by photographs of the Tasmanian wilderness when he was a child in Eastern Europe. Many years later he migrated to Australia, and every summer he would take months off work to go walking and exploring in the land that he loved. He had no formal qualifications — he painted buildings for most of the year — but his work as an amateur botanist was so highly respected that he had a species named after him. He even starred in a documentary about the wilderness. He followed his heart, and he made a lasting contribution to humanity's appreciation of the natural world.

When you act from love you give the world a gift of love. A house built with love is a joy to enter; food grown with love nourishes the spirit. And even if you 'fail' your efforts will not have been in vain, because love is its own reward and all action that springs from love creates energy for positive change.

What is love? This is one of the most profound questions in life. Some scientists believe that love is a biochemical phenomenon or a behavioural by-product of evolution. But love is something far greater than this, something without which our goals and achievements pale into insignificance. We may have the most elaborate technology, the most elegant philosophies and the most enthralling entertainments; but if we have no love, our lives will be shallow and meaningless. Love is our greatest gift and the highest expression of our humanity.

We feel love's power when we are 'in love' – that enchanted state that so easily fades when reality frustrates our desires. We come close to love in moments of joy and exaltation, moments when we are awed by the wonder of the universe.

Such moments are rare. But if you are aware, you can sense the intimations of love in your daily life, when you are sitting on a bus or walking down a city street. It is as if a fire is lit in your heart, a fire that nothing can extinguish. That fire gives you the energy to face all sorts of setbacks and difficulties.

A passion for the wild

Suprabha Seshan

WESTERN GHATS, INDIA

As a child I discovered a passion for nature at a time when no-one else I knew felt that way. But I had excellent role models in adults who were uncompromising in their concern for the world. I grew up in Delhi but when I was seven my family spent a year in Panama, and it was there that I first remember being fascinated by nature: jungles, macaws and looming volcanoes.

When I was eleven my parents enrolled me in the Valley School, a Krishnamurti school that had just opened on the outskirts of Bangalore in southern India. The school, which had an extraordinarily liberal ethos, was situated on a hundred acres of the wildest country I had ever seen. I spent a lot of my time there going for long walks, catching snakes and playing in the savannah scrub. At night we could hear jackals and see big horned owls. I fell in love with the natural world, its wild energies and endless beauty. I also grew to love the spaces that emerged inside me when I was alone with wild things.

When the time came for me to choose another high school, I chose the Krishnamurti school at Rishi Valley because of its natural setting. I got into fairly big-time exploration there (at least by city kid standards), hiking and bird watching in the surrounding hills. Most of the time there were just two or three of us; and the nice thing was that although the school was strict in many ways, nobody stood guard over us or told us we couldn't go off by ourselves.

In those days I thought of Krishnamurti as a teasing, friendly grandfather. I only spoke with him on rare occasions, but he struck me as someone you could say anything to, which was so different from most other adults I'd met. He also invited questioning and argument – and we kids were very argumentative! One day a group of us ambushed him and asked if we could meet him sometime. He twinkled back, 'Absolutely, let's go for a walk'. So we did, and our long walk was full of humour, questions and shared observations of that ancient landscape. (The rocks in Rishi Valley have been dated at over two billion years old.) He then invited us to lunch, and it was there that we discussed the possibility of some of us going as mature students to Brockwood Park School in England.

Two of us went to Brockwood Park because we were full of questions about the world and we

wanted to be with other people who were inquiring with equal passion. We both desperately wanted to study wildlife but we weren't inspired by the academic courses available in India at that time. We had written away to David Attenborough and Gerald Durrell – the only people we could think of! – and they basically said, 'Grow up a bit and then write again'! David Attenborough was very sweet and supportive, and Gerald Durrell sent signed photographs of himself holding chimpanzees!

I was eighteen when I went to Brockwood. During my first year there I worked in the garden, went on endless walks in the Hampshire countryside and took courses in philosophy, social development, gender and poverty. I then enrolled in the Open University and took courses in life sciences and Third World studies. I began to get bored with the Hampshire countryside because you couldn't see a lizard or a snake, and the most dangerous thing was a bee! But at the same time I wanted to understand whichever environment I was in. Then one of the staff members told me about a project offered by the Hampshire County Council, which was to undertake a historical study of the Brockwood Park estate. We decided to turn it into a study of its ecological history, which was fascinating because during the previous two centuries every management regime at Brockwood had reflected what was happening in the larger landscape of England.

Over the next two years I got to know every nook and cranny of Brockwood, and I also got to know people in the neighbourhood who'd had great aunts working at Brockwood as maids or uncles working as chauffeurs. I became fascinated with the history of the land and its people, the changes that had taken place over time, and what it might be like in the future. That study, more than anything I did with the Open University, was crucial in helping me to understand what it meant to be related to a particular area and to have a sense of place.

'I grew to love the spaces that emerged inside me when I was alone with wild things.'

By the time I graduated from the Open University I did not want to go on studying. So I hit upon the idea of travelling to explore wilderness and how people related to wilderness. While I was making plans I ran into a good friend who said, 'If you want any air tickets just let me know'. I created a kind of a self-study program and asked five people to referee the project – people I respected and who I knew would challenge me.

I travelled intensively for about eight months – in India, Nepal, Malaysia, Thailand, the European Alps and some of the wilder parts of Britain. Wherever I went I explored natural landscapes and investigated local attitudes to them. Often I did this simply by talking to people on buses or in the street. Many of the people I talked with said they would like to have a closer relationship with nature, but almost invariably they would add that they'd been forced to make choices that prevented this. I found this quite disturbing because it seemed that so many people were taking a soft option, often with disastrous consequences for themselves and for their communities and landscapes.

In 1992 I accepted a ten-month internship at the Land Institute in Kansas, where a small group of scientists were – and still are – designing an agro-ecosystem based on the natural principles of the prairie. I was one of eight students, and we had great fun romping around the prairies and meeting well-known writers and teachers like Wendell Berry and David Orr. The following year, I found my true vocation – ironically, just a few hours' drive from my home in Bangalore. Situated on the edge of one of India's few remaining areas of tropical rainforest, the Gurukula Botanical Sanctuary is a forest garden where native plants are being cultivated for species and ecosystem restoration. It is also an educational centre, an organic farm and an alternative community whose members are devoted to inquiring into right living. As it happened, the staff there were looking for someone to help out. I joined with the intention of staying for six months, but I was soon captivated by the dark magic of the forest and by the beauty and bounty of tropical nature.

The Sanctuary was founded in 1981 by a man called Wolfgang Theuerkauf. Wolfgang grew up in the slums of Berlin, travelled to India and lived alone in the forest for many years. The story goes that one day he noticed a strange-looking orchid that had fallen out of a tree. When it stayed alive for weeks, he wondered how a plant could live without soil. Then he started noticing other strange things, and suddenly the whole diversity of the forest came alive for him. Wolfgang knew nothing about botany or gardening; he learnt purely by observation, and is now one of the leading authorities on native plants in India. One of the things that intrigued me when I first came to the Sanctuary was the amount of time people here spent in just going around and observing things. Most of the people here have no formal education, yet the work of the Sanctuary is now respected internationally.

There are six full-time workers here and another dozen or so people who come in every day from the neighbourhood. We have about 2000 species in cultivation, which is nearly half of all the known plant species in the Western Ghats bioregion. Wild plants are doing extremely well here, which is unusual in this country. Very few people study wild plants in India, which is a shame because there's so little forest left and the whole Ayurvedic industry, with its hundreds of medicines, is dependent on the forest. Our aim is not only to help conserve species but to restore entire plant communities in degraded areas.

Although we're out in one of the remotest and least developed parts of Kerala, we feel very connected to the rest of the world. It constantly amazes me that I'm meeting a wider cross-section of people here than I met in all my travels. In the dry season we get a constant stream of visitors ranging from schoolchildren and local farmers to conservationists, businesspeople and scientists. We've hosted groups of young people for up to three months, and in 2002 we were invited to send a representative to a conference in Australia. Yet during the monsoon months we have long periods when we're just a small group of friends alone in the forest and the rain.

Suprabha Seshan

12. Integrity

Integrity is the clarity of intention that comes with understanding and love.

How are we to live in this world, with all its problems and complexities? How can we ensure that, at the very least, our actions will not add to the world's problems? Rather, how can we contribute to making the world a better place?

In a world of more than six billion people it is easy to think, 'Nothing I do will make any difference'. We might concede that some people *do* make a difference, but regard them as the chosen few. Such thinking is misguided because every one of us is 'chosen'. We are all taking part in the human journey and for this very reason, every one of us is responsible for the fate of humanity.

We might say that we are not responsible for violence. Yet most of us vote for governments that maintain armed forces, which are instruments of violence. The governments of countries that possess nuclear weapons maintain the capacity to rain death on tens of millions of people at the flick of a few switches. And most of these governments are in power because people like you and me put them there.

The twentieth century illustrated all too graphically that ordinary people can be responsible for horrifying crimes. The systematic murder of six million Jews in Germany between 1938 and 1945 cannot be blamed entirely on the upper echelons of the Nazi regime. It was a catastrophic moral failure on the part of an educated, economically developed and nominally Christian society. In 1934 ninety percent of Germans approved Hitler's assumption of dictatorial power, and he continued to enjoy widespread support as the Nazi persecution of Jews and other minorities escalated.

How can the thoughts and actions of one 'ordinary' person affect the world? Consider the simple example of dishwashing detergent. Everyone knows we shouldn't pour environmentally damaging chemicals down the sink. But if I use non-biodegradable detergent, what difference will it make? After all, I am only one person in a community of thousands or millions. The amount I pour down the sink may not even be measurable by the time it reaches the nearest river. Why should I bother to do the right thing?

For a start, my choice *will* make a physical difference, regardless of whether it is measurable. I may be contributing (albeit a thousandth of one percent) towards the outbreak of an algal bloom. My negligence may be the final straw that drives a species of fish to extinction.

Moreover, not all the consequences of my irresponsibility get flushed into the sewers and seas. The state of mind that I bring to buying detergent will be more or less the same state of mind that I bring to all my relationships. If I am unscrupulous when I do the washing-up I am likely to be unscrupulous in other aspects of my life; and every time I am unscrupulous I am betraying my fellow human beings, the planet and ultimately myself. Society can only function to the extent that each of us thinks and acts in a moral way. If we are deceitful and inconsiderate, even though our actions may seem insignificant in the overall scheme of things, our political and economic institutions will inevitably be dysfunctional and corrupt. If we live irresponsibly there will inevitably be global disorder.

Conversely, even a single act of integrity can have an enormous impact because all of us, in our heart of hearts, yearn to live with integrity, and we are inspired when we see examples of it in other people's lives. Three days after the September 11, 2001 terrorist attacks in New York and Washington, the United States Congress voted to grant President Bush unprecedented powers to use 'all necessary and appropriate force' in response to the attack. The vote was unanimous — nearly. Out of 98 senators and 421 House representatives, one person, Congresswoman Barbara Lee, cast a dissenting vote. She did so because she felt that military action would not prevent further acts of terrorism, and that the bill would give a 'blank cheque' to the president to wage war without consulting Congress or the American people. Given the level of emotion in the United States at that time, her lone stand must have taken extraordinary courage; yet in acting as she did she represented the feelings of millions of people in America and around the world. Even among her political opponents there were many who respected the integrity of her stand.

Integrity, by its very nature, asks for no reward; yet when you live with integrity your life has greater beauty and meaning. To be preoccupied with oneself and insensitive to other living beings is ultimately a lonely and miserable state. A person who is self-absorbed may have many pleasures, but lurking beneath them there is the agony of isolation and the inevitable dread of death. Surely happiness lies in the feeling that you are part of the flow of life; it comes from a sense of connection with your fellow human beings and the feeling that you are contributing something positive to the world.

To live with integrity is to be integrated, which means not fragmented within oneself. Most of us are fragmented because there is conflict between how we live and how, deep inside, we know we ought to live. We can be free of this conflict when we see that responsibility is not a burden to be carried, but a holistic action born of love. If you care for the Earth you will no sooner pour poisons down the sink than you would pour them into your morning coffee. When you see the vital importance of peace — not just

in your own neighbourhood or nation, but in the world — your life becomes a
journey on the path of peace.

Integrity is the clarity of intention that comes with understanding and love.

Achieving peace

O s c a r   A r i a s

COSTA RICA

I was a young boy when President José Figueres declared peace to the world by abolishing the Costa Rican army. The move was one of the many reforms he enacted in 1948, along with the extension of voting rights to women and full citizenship rights to black Costa Ricans. Since then I have had the privilege of living in a land that does not know tanks, attack helicopters or missiles, but instead enjoys one of the highest standards of social welfare in Latin America and one of the best standards of health care in the world.

The usual historical explanation for Costa Rica's stability and prosperity is that, owing to the lack of indigenous populations and large mineral deposits to exploit, Costa Rica's early colonisers had to work the land themselves. This produced a relatively egalitarian society that was more conducive to democracy than the highly stratified societies that developed in other Latin American countries. It would be simplistic to paint Costa Rica as a communal paradise, for we too have taken part in armed conflicts – both internal and external – and certainly our democracy is far from perfect. But the fact remains that Costa Rica today receives a constant stream of immigrants from nearby countries, most of which are locked in poverty and still suffering from the legacy of oppressive military regimes.

I can say without reservation that President Figueres' decision to abolish the army is the single most important explanation of Costa Rica's 'differentness'. In the immediate aftermath of the Cold War, many political commentators spoke of a hoped-for 'peace dividend'; that is, money that governments would no longer be spending on maintaining huge arsenals could be put to better use. While much of the world has not seen this benefit materialise, Costa Rica has been spending its peace dividend since 1948. Because we are a small country in a region often afflicted with violence and strife, dismantling our army was not an empty gesture. But we took the risk, and have since been able to pursue the path to development unencumbered by a bloated military establishment.

Perhaps the most immediate and obvious fruit of demilitarisation has been the political stability that Costa Rica has enjoyed, in contrast to the chaotic ups and downs that have been endured by all of our neighbours. Over the past fifty years, the military has intervened in the politics of every

other Central American country at one point or another, with disastrous results. In Guatemala, military regimes brutally decimated indigenous communities in a heavy-handed effort to crush a long-running insurgency. In Panama, the military governments were notoriously corrupt. Honduras, too, was ruled by military dictators for a long period of time, while Somoza relied on his National Guard to maintain his undemocratic regime in Nicaragua. And in El Salvador in the 1980s, military and paramilitary death squads had a profoundly destructive impact on the political life of that country. By contrast, demilitarised Costa Rica has maintained its democratic tradition throughout the past half-century: every four years, power has been transferred peacefully from one adminis- tration to the next.

The conviction of the Costa Rican people that war is not a solution allowed me as president to take bold steps to prevent the conflicts of neighbouring countries from spilling over into Costa Rica. When I took office in 1986, Costa Rica was already under great pressure from the US to allow its territory to be used for the training and equipping of the Contra forces of Nicaragua. Refusing to sacrifice Costa Rica's sovereignty and neutrality may have earned me enemies in Washington, but I have always had more faith in the negotiating table than the battlefield and my conscience was clear. Five Central American presidents held the fate of some thirty million people in our hands, and the responsibility was too great for us to walk away without an agreement. Ultimately our efforts at negotiating an accord were successful, although I was branded a naïve utopian for believing that the revolutionary government in Nicaragua would hold free elections, as they committed to doing when they signed the peace plan. Those who called themselves realists claimed that military victory was the only way to end the conflict in Central America. The realists were wrong. There is a first time for everything.

'Costa Rica is living proof that a nation can thrive without arms, tanks and fighter jets.'

Another major benefit of demilitarisation is that we have been able to direct a high percentage of our gross national product to health and education. Costa Rica has a quality public health care system that covers all of our people, as well as a private health insurance system that complements the services offered in public hospitals and clinics. The country boasts a life expectancy of 76 years, on a par with the US and Europe. By contrast, the average Guatemalan can expect to live only 65 years. On child health indicators, such as low birth-weight babies and infant immunisations, our numbers are virtually the same as those of the US, and on some health indicators, such as smoking and AIDS, we are doing better.

By investing in hospitals and doctors we can make our lives long and healthy, but in order to make our lives productive, we need education. Costa Rica's first head of state, elected in 1824, was a teacher, and I believe this prefigured the Costa Rica of today, in which we do not have an army of soldiers but rather an army of educators. Today, Costa Rica spends 5.4 percent of its gross national product on education, while the average for the other Central American countries, excluding Panama, is just 2.9 percent. When I accepted the Nobel Peace Prize in 1987 I called Costa Rica a land of teachers, where our children walk with books under their arms rather than guns on their shoulders. For over 130 years education has been free and compulsory in Costa Rica. Our adult literacy rate exceeds 95 percent, and nearly all of our children are enrolled in primary school.

We still need to make more progress: only around 65 percent of our adolescents are in high school, and not more than 15 percent attend university. This is partly because a large portion of our economy is still agrarian, and many rural young people forego secondary and tertiary education in order to take up the agricultural work their families have done for generations. However, technology and communications are changing the face of the Costa Rican economy – as well as nearly every other economy in the world – and we must increase our efforts to improve our educational system in order to effectively address that reality and ensure a brighter future for our youth.

The abolition of Costa Rica's armed forces in 1948, and the peace agreement that we reached in 1987, established Costa Rica as a global symbol of peace. But my country is not just a symbol; it is living proof that a nation can thrive without arms, tanks and fighter jets. We know that peace is not a utopia, nor solely a matter of agreements on paper. Peace is an ongoing commitment, a process, a way of life. It requires vigilance, patience and faith, and I am proud to have had the chance to represent my country in the exercise of those qualities, in order to share the benefits of our long-standing peaceful tradition with our neighbours in Central America.

The successes of Costa Rica stretch beyond its borders and the achievements of 1948 and 1987. For example, the Arias Foundation for Peace and Human Progress convinced both Panama and Haiti to officially disarm in the 1990s. Panama constitutionally abolished its army in 1994 and Haiti enacted a de facto abolition in 1996 when it reduced its military budget to zero.

The past has proven that Costa Rica can play a significant role in promoting peace and disarmament to its fellow nations, and I am certain that our positive role in the world will continue well into the future. We can share our emphasis on health and education in public spending, our forward-thinking environmental policies, our commitment to strong democratic institutions, and our embrace of resolving conflicts through negotiation. In the light of our history, beliefs and ideals, we can and should – indeed must – continue contributing to the creation of a more just and peaceful world.

Oscar Arias

Notes and resources

- The personal accounts by Ibrahim Alex Bangura and others are based on transcripts of interviews that I conducted in 2002. I interviewed Helen Thomas in person and Dr Oscar Arias in writing; the remaining ten interviews were conducted by telephone. The interviewees received drafts of their accounts for comment and review.
- Economic data throughout the text are in US dollars unless other currencies are indicated.
- I have used standard terms such as 'Third World' 'the South' and 'developed countries' throughout, while recognising that these terms are ideologically loaded and inevitably simplistic.
- All the Internet addresses cited below were valid on 18/3/2003.
- Where dates are expressed digitally, the format is dd/mm/yy.
- For additional information and links, see www.twelveprinciples.net. This website includes a discussion form.

Introduction

Page 10 ' … shortages of vital resources … '

For example water and arable land. Already one-third of the world's people live in regions where water is in short supply. (Source: World Resources Institute, *World Resources 2000–2001*, cited in the *AAAS Atlas of population and the environment*, www.ourplanet.com). By 2035 more than half of us may do so. (UN, quoted in *The Guardian* 25/5/02). Ten to twenty percent of the world's 1.5 billion hectares of cropland have already been degraded to some degree. (Worldwatch Institute 2002, *Vital Signs 2002–2003*, Earthscan, London.)

Page 10 ' … catastrophic disruptions affecting the lives of billions of people … '

For example, desertification threatens the livelihoods of more than a billon people. Source: Worldwatch Institute 2002, *Vital Signs 2002–2003*, Earthscan, London.

Page 10 'More than two billion people are already destitute … '

2.8 billion people have an income less than $2 a day. (Source: UNDP, *Global Human Development Report 2002*.) I am not suggesting that wealth can be measured exclusively in dollar terms; some nomadic people, for example, may have minimal incomes yet be socially and spiritually wealthy and have all they need materially. But the majority of people living on less than $2 a day suffer material deprivation such as inadequate housing, nutrition, sanitation and health services. According to UN figures, for example, more than a billion people live in slums or squatter settlements. (Source: *Guardian Weekly* 17–23/1/02.)

1. One people

Page 15 'In the late 1990s I spent a year at a school … '

Brockwood Park School in Hampshire, UK. The school is one of several founded by J. Krishnamurti (see chapter 7, below), but is the only such school in Europe. See www.brockwood.org.uk.

Page 16 'On Christmas Day in 1914 … '

See for example Malcolm Brown and Shirley Seaton's 1994, *Christmas Truce: The Western Front December 1914*, Papermac, Basingstoke.

Page 16 ' … let us also blacklist people and nations … '

The issues raised in this sentence are discussed at greater length in chapter 8.

Page 16 'In May 2000 a quarter of a million non-Aboriginal Australians … '

Sydney Morning Herald 29/5/00.

Page 16 ' … the wealthiest 20 percent of the world's population were 80 times richer than their counterparts in the poorest 20 percent.'

Source: *The Guardian* 11/5/98. Estimates vary depending on how they are calculated. According to Oxfam, a child born in Australia will have a lifetime income 74 times that of a child born in the developing world (Oxfam Community Aid Abroad 2001, *The Globalisation Challenge*, August).

Page 16 ' ... more than a billion people on Earth lack access to water that's safe to drink.'

Source: Statement by the United Nations Population Fund at the World Summit on Sustainable Development, Johannesburg, 2002. See www.un.org/events/wssd/statements/unfpaE.htm.

Page 18 ' ... efforts to restrict greenhouse gas emissions have been undermined ... '

The USA, Australia and major oil corporations were instrumental in sabotaging efforts to reduce greenhouse gases at the 2002 World Summit on Sustainable Development in Johannesburg. See for example *The Village News* 27/9/02 at http://villagenews.weblogger.com/stories/storyReader$6145.

Page 18 'An organisation called Seeds of Peace ... '

See www.seedsofpeace.org. The quote is taken from http://usembassy.state.gov/islamabad/wwwh01071803.html.

Page 18 'Greenpeace, Amnesty International and Global Greens ... '

See www.greenpeace.org, www.amnesty.org, www.global.greens.org.au.

Page 18 'The campaign to cancel Third World debt ... '

In the 1990s Jubilee 2000, a coalition of aid agencies and other NGOs, successfully lobbied the governments of the world's major industrialised nations to reduce the debt burden of the world's poorest countries. However, a debt-relief strategy agreed by the G7 nations in 1999 was not fully honoured and many of the world's poorest countries are still paying a substantial proportion of their budgets to the West to service debts. The debt-relief campaign is continuing under the banner Jubilee Movement International. Sources: www.jubilee2000uk.org; *Guardian Weekly* 23–29/1/03.

Page 19 'The village of Hawkshead ... '

Guardian Weekly 27/2/03–5/3/03.

Page 19 'In Afghanistan, a quarter of all children die before the age of five.'

Guardian Weekly 3–9/1/02, citing UN data.

Page 19 'In Zambia, Aids is killing almost as many teachers ...'

Guardian Weekly Earth supplement, Aug 2002.

Page 19 'In China, factory workers are labouring up to 16 hours a day ... '

Source: *Guardian Weekly* 23–29/5/02. The article referred in particular to migrant workers (primarily workers who have migrated from country areas to cities), who by some estimates number 200 million.

Page 19 ' ... people killed or "disappeared" by the Pinochet regime ... '

See for example Tito Tricot, 'The disappeared are still missing' in *Guardian Unlimited* 9/1/01 (www.guardian.co.uk/Archive).

Ibrahim Alex Bangura – Songs of healing

Page 20 ' ... by the year 2000 Sierra Leone was at the very bottom of the United Nations human-development list'

UNDP, *Global Human Development Report 2000*. See for example www.twf.org/News/Y2000/1010-HDI.pdf.

Page 22 Convention on the Rights of the Child

See www.unhchr.ch/html/menu3/b/k2crc.htm.

2. One planet

Page 24 'Scientists are investigating the prospect ... '

For example at Nasa. See P. Cohen 2000, 'Terraforming Mars: A NASA meeting on making the Red Planet habitable', October; *New Scientist* 2002 Online Conference Reports, www.newscientist.com/conferences. See also *New Scientist* 5/2/94 and 'Plants glow to Mars' [sic] in *Guardian Unlimited* 3/5/01 (www.guardian.co.uk/Archive).

Page 24 ' ... we may eventually be able to emigrate en masse to Mars.'

Several claims to this effect appeared in the media during the 1990s, for example in *The Australian* 20/7/94 (supplement). It's a dangerous idea because it suggests that humans have an escape clause: If we waste this planet, we can solve the problem by moving to another one. But the hard fact is, for the foreseeable future we're stuck with the Earth, and if we destroy it the game is over. In their book *Naked Ape to Superspecies* (Allen & Unwin, Sydney, 1999), David Suzuki and Holly Dressel make a similar argument by describing the Biosphere 2 project – a failed attempt to create an artificial, hermetically sealed ecosystem in Arizona.

Page 24 'But that is unlikely to be practical for millennia, if ever.'

See for example N. Nadis 1994, 'Mars, the final frontier', *New Scientist* 141:1911, Feb 5.

Page 24 'Every year the world is losing 24 billion tonnes of topsoil ... '

Source: H. Bakker (Ed) 1990, *The World Food Crisis: Food Security in Comparative Perspective*, Canadian Scholars Press, Toronto.

Page 24 ' … and an area of forest the size of England and Wales.'

Estimates of global forest loss vary depending on data sources, definitions of forest etc. The UN puts the figure at 14.6m hectares per year (*The Guardian* 9/1/02). The combined area of England and Wales is approximately 15 million hectares.

Page 24 'More than half the world's seventeen major fishing grounds have been severely depleted … '

Source: Greenpeace, citing the US Food and Agriculture Organisation, *Review of the State of the World Fishery Resources*, 1995.

See http://archive.greenpeace.org/~usa/reports/biodiversity/sinking_fast.

Page 24 ' … global temperatures could rise by up to 5.8°C … '

J. T. Houghton et al (eds), *Climate change 2001: The scientific basis*, Contribution of Working Group 1 to the Third Assessment Report of the Intergovernmental Panel on Climate Change, CUP, Cambridge UK.

Page 24 'Extreme weather events … '

According to the Intergovernmental Panel on Climate Change, increased droughts are 'likely' over most mid-latitude continental interiors, more intense precipitation events are 'very likely' over many areas, and tropical cyclones are 'likely' to become more intense over some areas. Source: IPCC 2001; R.T. Watson, and the Core Writing Team (eds.), *Climate Change 2001: Synthesis Report. A Contribution of Working Groups I, II, and III to the Third Assessment Report of the Intergovernmental Panel on Climate Change*, Cambridge University Press, Cambridge, UK, and New York, USA. See www.ipcc.ch.

Page 24-25 'There is a risk that global warming could release … '

This statement, and the quote by Britain's Environment Minister Michael Meacher, were taken from an article in *The Guardian* on 14/2/03, based on a lecture that Mr Meacher delivered at Newcastle University in February 2003. See www.guardian.co.uk/comment/story/0,3604,895217,00.html.

Page 25 'We can insert human genes into pigs … '

New Scientist 18/6/94.

Page 26 'In 2002 the city authorities of Tokyo … '

New York Times 13/8/02.

Jill Redwood – The fight for the forests

Page 28 'The East Gippsland area contains the most diverse range … 15 football fields every day.'

Sources: The Wilderness Society
(www.wilderness.org.au/member/tws/projects/Forests/egippsland.html) and Concerned
Residents for East Gippsland (http://home.vicnet.net.au/~croeg/). For original sources and further
information see the CROEG website or contact the Wilderness Society (www.wilderness.org.au).

3. Responsibility

Page 32 'The simple act of buying a shirt … '

For information about fair (and unfair) trade practices see for example www.fairtradefed-
eration.com or www.globalexchange.org. See also chapter 10.

Page 33 ' … politicians or their corporate sponsors … '

In the 2000 US election cycle, corporations donated a total of $1.2 billion in political contri-
butions – 14 times the contributions of labour unions and 16 times those of other interest
groups. In India, large corporations provided 80 percent of the funding for the major political
parties in 1996. (Source: UNDP, *Global Human Development Report 2002.*)

In 2002 the US Congress approved a bill that will restrict the amount of money that
individuals or corporations can donate to political parties or candidates. (Source: *The Guardian*
22/3/02.) It remains to be seen how this reform will affect the link between corporate money
and political influence in the United States.

Page 33 ' … such as oil companies and arms manufacturers … '

In 2002, oil and gas industries donated $17m to the Republican Party congressional elections
and $2m to George W Bush's election campaign. The industry was subsequently rewarded
with rollbacks on environmental regulations. For example, in November 2002 the US
Environmental Protection Agency allowed 17,000 old coal-fired power stations, oil refineries
and factories to expand or renovate without installing pollution filters as previously required.
(Source: *Guardian Weekly* 23–29/1/03, citing the Centre for Responsive Politics.)

Between 1991 and 1997, defence companies donated more than $30m to US political
parties and candidates. (Source: Centre for Responsive Politics, cited in Hartung WD 1999,
'Military-industrial complex revisited: How weapons makers are shaping US foreign and
military policies', *Foreign policy in focus*, August; see www.foreignpolicy-infocus.org).

Angie Zelter – Denting the sword

Page 36 The ten women involved in planning and carrying out the Hawk jet action were Lyn Bliss, Claire Fearnley, Emily Johns, Lotte Kronlid, Andrea Needham, Rowan Tilly, Ricarda Steinbrecher, Jen Parker, Joanna Wilson and Angie Zelter. Of the ten, Lotte Kronlid, Andrea Needham, Joanna Wilson and Angie Zelter each spent six months in jail awaiting trial.

The two women who took part with Ms Zelter in damaging the research laboratory were Ulla Roder and Ellen Moxley.

For information on the Trident Ploughshares campaign see www.tridentploughshares.org. For information on Angie's current work in Palestine see www.womenspeacepalestine.org.

Page 36 ' ... a 1996 opinion by the International Court of Justice ... '

ICJ 1996, 'Legality of the Threat or Use of Nuclear Weapons', *Advisory Opinion*, July 8 1996. (Reports 1996, p. 226). The ICJ used the phrase 'weapons that are incapable of distinguishing between civilian and military targets'.

Page 38 The Ecologist

The Ecologist is a UK-based magazine devoted to the coverage of environmental, social and economic issues. See www.theecologist.org.

4. Making a difference

Page 40 ' ... a young Canadian called Craig Kielburger ... '

See www.freethechildren.com, and in particular
http://www.freethechildren.com/info/aboutcraig.html.

Page 40 'The Indian activist Jaya Arunachalam ... '

See www.workingwomensforum.org.

Page 40 ' ... Visheswar Saklani started planting trees ... '

Source: *Earth Island Journal* 13:1, Winter 97–98. See
http://www.earthisland.org/eijournal/win98/wr_win98greenpages.html.

Page 41 'When Australia's fledgling Wilderness Society ... '

See for example Peter Thompson 1984, *Bob Brown of the Franklin River*, Allen & Unwin, Sydney. For current information on the Wilderness Society see www.wilderness.org.au.

Page 41 'You don't have to be an activist.'

And becoming an activist won't necessarily help to solve the world's problems. If you are aggressive and factional you may do more harm than good.

Page 42 'Roberto Arévalo teaches teenagers ... '

See www.mirrorproject.org.

Page 42 '**On the day in 1991 that Britain's former Prime Minister Margaret Thatcher stepped down from office ... '**

Source: *Weekend Australian* 6–7/4/91. In the UK the monarch bestows knighthoods on the advice of the prime minister.

Rowenna Davis – The writing on the wall

Page 44 For more information about the Messengers campaign see www.messengers.org.uk/index2.htm; see also www.messengers.org.uk. For information on the Johannesburg Earth Summit (officially known as the World Summit on Sustainable Development) see www.johannesburgsummit.org and www.guardian.co.uk/worldsummit2002/0,12264,757397,00.html.

The statements on the ten posters were as follows:

- If everyone in the world consumed as much as the average American, eight additional planets would be needed to sustain the consumption.
- During the 20th century three-quarters of agricultural genetic diversity was lost.
- By the time you read this, five US football pitches worth of rainforest would have been destroyed.
- On average, sperm count has decreased by 50% in the last 50 years.
- 20% of the world consume 86% of the world's resources.
- One billion people are hungry today.
- One quarter of all people don't have water today.
- 25% of the world's animals and 11% of its birds are at risk of extinction.
- There is a hole in the ozone layer three times the size of the USA.
- Six billion tonnes of carbon dioxide are released every year through the burning of fossil fuels.

5. Learning

Page 51 '**In 2002 a survey in Belfast ... '**

Guardian Weekly 10–16/1/02.

Venu – Learning in freedom

Page 54 'Venu' is Venu's personal name. He has degrees in engineering and management, and he worked for many years in the private business sector.

The Centre for Learning website is www.cfledu.org.

6. Seeing

Page 60 'The advocates of economic rationalism … '

For example:

- In a speech to the Royal Society in London in May 2002, British Prime Minister Tony Blair referred to opponents of genetic engineering as 'protestors and pressure groups who [use] emotion to drive out reason'. (Source: *Guardian Unlimited* 23/5/02, http://politics.guardian.co.uk/speeches/story/0,11126,721029,00.html.)
- In 2001 the US Interior Secretary Bruce Babbitt described environmentalists opposed to nuclear energy as 'deeply irrational' (Science and Environment Policy Project, *The Week That Was* 29/9/2001, www.sepp.org/weekwas/2001/sept29.htm).
- The American political commentator George F Will has described the political left as 'little other than an amalgam of baby-boomer nostalgia and moral vanity' (*Pittsburgh Tribune-Review* 23/1/03, www.pittsburghlive.com/x/tribune-review/opinion/will/s_114156.html).

7. Self-awareness

Page 68 J. Krishnamurti

As a child and young man, Krishnamurti (1895–1986) was groomed by the Theosophical Society to be the new World Teacher. In 1929 he renounced this role, claiming that 'Truth is a pathless land' and rejecting all organised religions and sects. He spent the rest of his life giving talks and participating in dialogues around the world. See for example his *Commentaries on Living (Series 1–3)*, Theosophical Publishing House, 1994.

Page 68 Ramana Maharshi

Ramana Maharshi (1879–1950), formerly called Venkataraman, underwent a profound spiritual transformation at the age of sixteen. Shortly afterwards he left his home and travelled to the town of Tiruvannamalai in southern India, where he spent the remainder of his life. He gave private audiences and talks, many of which were recorded. See for example D. Godman's (ed) 1985, *Be as you are: The teachings of Ramana Maharshi*, Penguin Arcana, London.

Stephen Fulder – The transformation of suffering

Page 72 Sarvodaya movement

The Sarvodaya movement is a voluntary, nongovernment community development movement that began in Colombo in 1958 and has since spread throughout Sri Lanka and to other countries. See www.sarvodaya.org.

Page 72 'Our community developed along Gandhian lines … '

Mohandas Gandhi (1869–1948), who became widely known as 'Mahatma' (Great Soul), espoused the values of truth, nonviolence, universal brotherhood and humanitarian service. He was also a strong advocate of self-sufficiency. See for example www.mkgandhi.org.

Page 73 The Insight Society

The Insight Society runs courses and retreats on dharma and Buddhist meditation in Israel. Its website is in Hebrew (www.tovana.org.il); its email address is tovana@tovana.org.il.

Stephen Fulder is also involved with the peace group 'Shvil Zahav' ('Middle Way'). Its website is partly in English; see www.middleway.org.

Page 75 Hamas

Hamas is a grassroots Islamist organisation that has been responsible for terrorist attacks against Israelis. It has also undertaken community development work in the Palestinian territories. See for example http://news.bbc.co.uk/1/hi/world/middle_east/978626.stm.

8. Global awareness

Page 76 'The last twenty years have seen vast changes … '

For information about globalisation and its economic and environmental effects, see for example the Oxfam report *Rigged rules and double standards: Trade, globalisation and the fight against poverty*, which is available on the Oxfam website www.oxfam.org.hk/english/resource/publications/2002_1/01.pdf.

See *also* www.globalexchange.org.

Page 76 ' … the economic crisis of 1997 cut real wages in Indonesia … '

Oxfam Community Aid Abroad 2001, *The Globalisation Challenge*, August.

Page 76 ' … the collapse of the Ghanaian rice industry.'

Guardian Weekly 6–12/6/02.

Page 77 'Per capita incomes declined in more than eighty countries during the 1990s.'

Oxfam Community Aid Abroad 2001, *The Globalisation Challenge*, August.

Page 77 'Pressure from organisations like the International Monetary Fund ... has fuelled escalating environmental destruction ... '

For example, in 1998 pressure from the IMF led the Brazilian government to slash spending on a major rainforest conservation project. (Source: *The Guardian* 2/1/99.) The Care2 website provides excellent links on a wide range of issues relating to globalisation, including its environmental impacts – see http://www.care2.com/channels/ecoinfo/trade.

Page 77 'It is these governments that set the rules for global trade ... '

In the World Trade Organisation, for example, 'every member country has a seat and vote, which is very democratic. But actual decision-making occurs by consensus, heavily influenced by the largest and richest countries.' Quoted from: UNDP, *Global Human Development Report 2002.*

Page 77 ' ... protectionist laws are costing developing countries more than $100 billion per year ... '

The Guardian 11/4/02, citing Oxfam.

Page 77 ' ... aid budgets had dwindled to all-time lows ... '

Oxfam Horizons Aug 2001. US and European aid budgets were boosted in 2002 but the increases were largely offset by increased subsidies for wealthy farmers (*Guardian Weekly* 21–27/3/02; see also Nicholas D. Kristof, 'Farm subsidies that kill' in the *New York Times* 5/7/02). Moreover aid is often spent on projects that are of questionable environmental and social value, and that are primarily in the interests of donor governments – for example highways, dams, military infrastructure and the so-called war on drugs. See for example www.onlineopinion.com.au/June00/hobbs.htm.

Page 77 ' ... [the US] government's role in training and funding death squads ... '

For example in Guatamala (*Guardian Weekly* 7/7/96), Haiti (*Guardian Weekly* 10/12/95), Honduras (*Guardian Weekly* 29/10/95), Nicaragua (*Independent* 29/5/98), Mexico (*Guardian Weekly* 12/4/98) and Chile (Peter Kornbluh (ed) 2003, *The Pinochet File: A Declassified Dossier on Atrocity and Accountability*, National Security Archive).

For references to American involvement in death squads in more than 20 countries see http://serendipity.magnet.ch/cia/death_squads.htm.

Page 78 ' ... America's support for the 1975 Indonesian invasion of East Timor ... '

See for example *Guardian Weekly* 30/10/94; BBC News 7/12/01 (http://news.bbc.co.uk/1/hi/world/asia-pacific/1697248.stm).

The US administration gave tacit support in advance to the invasion, and continued to supply Indonesia with arms that were used against the East Timorese.

Source: W. Burr & M. Evans (eds) 2001, *National Security Archive Electronic Briefing Book No. 62*, Dec 6. See www.gwu.edu/~nsarchiv/NSAEBB/NSAEBB62.

Page 78 'One Tibetan monk, Palden Gyatso ... '

See for example Palden Gyatso 1997, *The Autobiography of a Tibetan Monk*, Grove, New York.

Page 78 ' ... hundreds of his compatriots remain in prison ... '

In 2002 131 000 Tibetans were living in exile (Source: Government of Tibet in Exile, www.tibet.com) and in 2001 there were approximately 300 documented political prisoners in Tibet (International Campaign for Tibet, www.savetibet.org).

Page 78 ' ... China's status as a "Most Favoured Nation" trading partner ... '

The Age (Melbourne) 3/2/95

Page 78 ' ... or prevent China's entry into the World Trade Organisation ... '

Guardian Unlimited 11/12/01 (www.guardian.co.uk/Archive).

Page 78 'Yet mainstream media have paid very little attention to what is happening in ... Chechnya, or Colombia ... '

See for example Human Rights Watch, www.hrw.org/campaigns/russia/chechnya and www.hrw.org/campaigns/colombia.

Page 78 ' ... or the Kurdish sector of Turkey ... '

Turkey has pursued a systematic policy of killings, forced migration and human rights abuses against the Kurds whilst receiving billions of dollars in American aid and military support. Up to 3000 villages have been wiped out in southeast Turkey since 1985 and two million Kurds have been forced to flee their homes. See for example *Guardian Weekly* 7/7/96; http://pilger.carlton.com/print/52580.

Page 78 ' ... the *Virgin Islands Daily News* ... '

The Age (Melbourne) 20/4/95. See also www.pulitzer.org/year/1995/public-service.

Page 80 ' ... commentators such as Noam Chomsky ... '

See for example Chomsky's *Rogue States: The Rule of Force in World Affairs*, Pluto, London, 2000.

Page 80 ' ... and John Pilger ... '

See for example Pilger's *The New Rulers of the World*, Verso, London, 2002.

Page 80 ' … you should talk to Jason Crowe … '

Jason Crowe's website is http://members.sigecom.net/jdc.

Joliz Cedeño – The wider world

Page 82 Beacon School

See www.beaconschool.org.

Page 83 Global Kids

See www.globalkids.org.

9. Respect

Page 89 'The members of many indigenous communities … '

See for example T. C. McLuhan (ed) 1993, *Touch the Earth: A self-portrait of Indian existence*, Abacus, London.

Page 89 ' … we kill animals on conveyor belts … '

Admittedly, the 'clinical' mass slaughter of cattle carries less risk of spreading BSE than traditional butchering techniques; see for example an article by Kevin Toolis in *The Guardian*, 22/9/01. Whether mechanised mass slaughter is humane remains open to question.

Page 89 ' … vCJD … which by 2003 had killed more than 120 people … '

As of January 2003 there had been 121 confirmed deaths due to vCJD in Britain. Source: UK Department of Health, http://www.doh.gov.uk/cjd/cjd_stat.htm.

Page 90 'One such program, YARD (Youth At Risk Dancing) … '

See www.cominguptaller.org/awards/program10.html.

Cathrine Sneed – Seeds of renewal

Page 95 'Three-quarters of our employees do not return to jail.'

A recidivism study published in *American Jails* magazine found that 55 percent of offenders released from San Francisco County Jail were rearrested within one year, while only 27 percent of Garden Project participants were rearrested within *four* years of their release. Source: Michael Hennessey, 'The dirt on stopping crime: Garden Project', *San Francisco Examiner* 29/6/99.

The Garden Project website is www.gardenproject.org.

10. Simplicity

Page 96 Mohandas Gandhi

See note under 'Stephen Fulder – The transformation of suffering' above.

Page 96 'Canadian researchers … '

Namely, William Rees and Mathis Wackernagel. (Source: W. Rees & M. Wackernagel 1996, *Our Ecological Footprint: Reducing Human Impact on Earth*, New Society Publishers, Gabriola Island, BC.) The estimate of 'eight additional planets' cited on one of the 'Messengers' posters (see 'Rowenna Davis – The writing on the wall', above) is probably based on projected increases in global population. See for example www.global-vision.org/city/footprint.html.

Page 96 'The world's richest 50 million people are collectively as wealthy as the poorest 2.7 billion people.'

And the poorest one-fifth of the world's population earn barely 1 percent of its income. Source: *Guardian Weekly* 24–30/1/02, citing World Bank economist Branko Milanovik in the Jan 2002 edition of *Economic Journal*.

Page 96 'Australia consumes 80 percent as much oil as Indonesia … '

In 2002 Australia and Indonesia consumed 870 000 and 1 065 000 barrels of oil per day, respectively. (Source: BP Amoco, www.geohive.com/charts/energy_oilcons.php.) The 2002 populations of Australia and Indonesia were 19.5 million and 231 million respectively. (Source: *CIA World Factbook 2002*, www.cia.gov/cia/publications/factbook).

Page 96 'The United States, with less than 5 percent of the world's population … '

For current US and world population figures see US Census Bureau, www.census.gov/main/www/popclock.html.

Page 96 ' … produces a quarter of the world's greenhouse gases'.

Worldwatch Institute 2002, *Vital Signs 2002–2003*, Earthscan, London.

Page 96 'The richest one-fifth of the world's population consume four-fifths of the planet's resources.'

Statement by the United Nations Population Fund at the World Summit on Sustainable Development, Johannesburg, 2002.

See www.un.org/events/wssd/statements/unfpaE.htm.

Page 96 'A 1998 United Nations report estimated … spend on pet food and cosmetics.'

Source: *The Guardian* 9/9/98, citing that year's UN *Human Development Report*.

Page 97 **'The abolition of subsidies ... The cancellation of Third World debts ... '**

See for example the Oxfam report *Rigged rules and double standards: Trade, globalisation and the fight against poverty*, which is available on the Oxfam website www.oxfam.org.hk/english/resource/publications/2002_1/01.pdf.

See also www.globalexchange.org.

Page 97 **' ... some [Third World nations] have been paying more on debt servicing than on health or education.'**

In 1999, Zambia was spending substantially more on debt servicing than on its health and education budget combined. In the same year, debt servicing exceeded the health or education budget (or both) in Tanzania, Mozambique, Nicaragua and Honduras. (Source: Jubilee 2000, www.jubilee2000uk.org/databank/data.htm.) According to Oxfam, this situation will continue for many countries even after recent debt-relief measures have been implemented. (Source: Oxfam Community Aid Abroad 2001, *The Globalisation Challenge*, August.)

Page 97 **'The American lifestyle is not up for negotiation' (Statement by President George Bush Snr on the eve of the 1992 Earth Summit in Rio de Janeiro).**

Time 1/6/92.

Page 98 **'Per capita wealth in industrialised countries has more than doubled ... '**

Most of the data in this paragraph are taken from A. L. Oswald, 'Happiness and Economic Performance' in the *Economic Journal*, November 1997. See also B. Frey and A. Stutzer, *Happiness and Economics: How the Economy and Institutions Affect Human Well-Being*, Princeton University Press, 2001.

Page 98 **'A greater gain in community wellbeing ... '**

America's 2002 military budget was $396 billion, or more than $1 billion a *day*. Source (with information on world military expenditures): Center for Defence Information, www.cdi.org.

Page 98 **'A survey conducted in 1989 ... '**

Source: *The Chivas Regal Report on Working Americans*, Research & Forecasts, New York City, 1989; cited in R. Henkoff 1989, 'Is greed dead?', *Fortune*, 14/8/89. In the same survey, workers were asked 'Which of the following would most give you the feeling of success in your life?' Only 10 percent chose the answer 'Earning lots of money' while 62 percent chose 'Happy family life'. (Source: *Inc* magazine 1/11/92. See www.inc.com/magazine/19921101/4386.html.)

Page 98 ' … advertisements exploit this feeling.'

For a thought-provoking critique of the advertising industry see the Adbusters website –
www.adbusters.org.

Page 99 'Around the world, thousands of people are already living in eco-villages … '

See for example www.ecovillages.org and http://gen.ecovillage.org.

Page 99 'In Nottinghamshire, England ... '

See www.hockerton.demon.co.uk.

Page 99 'Co-housing projects … '

See for example www.cohousing.ca.

Page 100 'Increasing numbers of people are subscribing to community-supported agriculture
… '

See for example www.umass.edu/umext/csa, www.localharvest.org/morecsa.jsp and the
Cathrine Sneed story in this book.

Page 100 'David Tagliani … '

Source: *Moscow Times* 28/09/01.

Page 100 'The traditional indicator of a nation's wealth … '

For a discussion of the inadequacies of GNP see for example D. Suzuki & H. Dressel 1999,
Naked Ape to Superspecies, Allen & Unwin, Sydney.

Page 100 'Economists are now beginning to develop measures of wealth … '

See for example *Briefing: Accounting for Change: The role of sustainable development
indicators*, Alex MacGillivray and Simon Zadek, New Economics Foundation,
http://www.sussex.ac.uk/Units/gec/pubs/briefing/brf-nef.htm; also
http://oikosinternational.org/centers_of_excellence/ami.

Page 100 'In Japan … local governments are introducing their own currencies … '

Source: *Guardian Weekly* 31/10/02–6/11/02.

Page 101 ' … the town of Garstang in Lancashire … '

See www.garstangoxfamgroup.fsnet.co.uk. For more information about fair trade see
www.fairtradefederation.com and www.globalexchange.org.

Christian Leppert – Sufficiency

Page 102 The website www.chooseclimate.org is an excellent source of information about
carbon emissions, particularly those associated with air travel. It includes an interactive global

climate model and information about the 'Climate train' from Europe to the 1997 climate summit in Kyoto. Several personal carbon-emission calculators are available on the Internet – although in my experience, not all of them work!

The Haus Sonne website address is www.haussonne.com.

11. Love

*Page 107 '***In parts of East Asia, children as young as two are being forced to sit for exams ... '**
For example in Japan. Source: World Socialist Web Site 19/6/00 (www.wsws.org/articles/2000/jun2000/jap-j19.shtml).

Page 107 ' **... and six-month-old babies are being sat in front of instructional videos ... '**
In South Korea. Source: *Guardian Weekly* 16–22/5/02.

Page 108 **'Some scientists believe that love is a biochemical phenomenon ... '**
See for example Spencer A. Rathus, *Essentials of Psychology*, Holt, Rinehart & Winston, Fort Worth, Texas, 1989; also *New Scientist* 29/1/94.

Suprabha Seshan – A passion for the wild

Page 110 ' **... my parents enrolled me in the Valley School ... '**
The Valley School, Rishi Valley School and Brockwood Park School were all founded by J. Krishnamurti – see note under chapter 7.

Page 113 **Ayurvedic medicine**
Ayurveda is a holistic system of healing that has been practised in India for at least 3000 years. See for example http://niam.com/corp-web/definition.html.

12. Integrity

*Page 114 '***The governments of countries that possess nuclear weapons ... '**
For information on America's nuclear-weapons capacity see www.brook.edu/FP/PROJECTS/NUCWCOST/50.HTM. For information on the capacity and destructive potential of Britain's Trident system see www.tridentploughshares.org.

*Page 115 '***In 1934 ninety percent of Germans ... '**
In March 1933, elections in Germany gave the Nazis (the National Socialist German Workers' Party) 44 percent of the vote and 288 of the 647 seats in the Reichstag (German parliament).

Shortly afterwards the Nazis used widespread intimidation to pass an Enabling Act, which effectively gave Hitler absolute power. (Source: G. Caldwell 2001, 'To what extent did Hitler come to power legally?', www.gregcaldwell.co.uk, Dundee, www.geocities.com/gregcaldwell/documents/power.htm.)

In August 1934 a national plebiscite indicated 89.9 percent support for the consolidation of Hitler's position as Führer (leader) of the Third Reich (German Empire). Sources: *New York Times*, 20/8/1934; R. Otmar, (ed) 2001, *SBS World Guide*, Hardie Grant, Melbourne.

The extent to which ordinary Germans knew about the Holocaust is still hotly debated. This question aside, there is abundant evidence that ordinary Germans knew the Nazis were persecuting Jews and other minorities. See for example E. Johnson 2000, *Nazi Terror: The Gestapo, Jews, and ordinary Germans*, John Murray, London.

Page 116 ' … Congresswoman Barbara Lee cast a dissenting vote.'
For Congresswoman Lee's statement on why she opposed the anti-terrorism bill, see www.commondreams.org/views01/0923-04.htm. Barbara Lee's website is www.house.gov/lee.

Oscar Arias – Achieving peace

Page 118 Dr Oscar Arias Sánchez was President of Costa Rica from 1986–1990 and was awarded the Nobel Peace Prize in 1987 for his work in brokering a five-nation peace accord in Central America. He used the prize money to establish the Arias Foundation for Peace and Human Progress, which is working to promote peace, justice and social development in Central America and other regions. See www.arias.or.cr/Eindice.htm.

Costa Rica is Spanish for 'Rich Coast', the name given to the country by Spanish colonisers who, observing that some of the natives wore gold decorations, imagined that there was a rich civilisation in the hinterland.

For further reading on Costa Rica see for example M. H. Biesanz and others 1998, *The Ticos: Culture and Social Change in Costa Rica*, Lynne Rienner Publishers, Boulder.

Photographic notes

All of Martin Hawes' images were taken in the Tasmanian Wilderness World Heritage Area.

Endpapers Children playing in a monsoon rainstorm, Bangladesh.
© M. Rahman/UNEP/Still Pictures

Page 4–5 Detail of liverwort leaf, Weld Valley. © Martin Hawes

Page 6 Dawn sky, moon and valley mist, Weld Valley.
© Martin Hawes

Page 11 Rock and reflected evening sky, Snowy Range.
© Martin Hawes

Page 12 Bird footprints in sand, Southwest Coast. © Martin Hawes

Page 17 Mixed-race school, Harare, Zimbabwe, 2001.
© David Reed/ Panos Pictures

Page 21 Ethnic dance school group, Gabarone, Botswana.
© Julio Etchart/Still Pictures

Page 27 Hiking in an old growth forest, Olympic National Park,
Washington, USA. © Kevin Schafer/Still Pictures

Page 29 Environmental road protestor in net during eviction,
Newbury bypass, UK. © Nick Cobbing/Still Pictures

Page 35 Refugees from degraded agricultural land, Borde de
Vias colony, Mexico City. © Mark Edwards/Still Pictures

Page 37 Trident Ploughshares activist being arrested during an
action. © B. P. Hill.

Page 43 Stranded whale, Florida beach, USA.
© Janet Jarman/Still Pictures

Page 45 Somali girl filling a water container from a pump
installed by Oxfam, Wajir, Northern Kenya.
© Adrian Arbib/Still Pictures

Acknowledgements

This book is the outcome of a writing project that began in the early 1990s, and I would like to thank everyone who contributed to its development. In particular I would like to say thanks:

To everyone who shared their stories of courage, integrity and hope;

To Mark Edwards and the Still Pictures photo library, for their invaluable contribution to this project;

To Ralph Barraclough, Chris Bell, Nick Coleson, Alison Connell, Louise Crossley, Mark Darby, Tracey Diggins, Iris Dillow, Barbara Fisher, Jeffrey Fisher, Graham Green, Mary Jenkins, Alan Kinsman, Satish Kumar, Margie Law, Cath Leith, Olga Maiboroda, Mary Anne Manigian, Ted Mead, Dagmar Nordberg, Verne Osborn, Kate Pile, Helen Thomas, Oliver Ward, Sally Ward, Chip Wardale, and Lilith Waud – for their comments, encouragement and constructive criticism on drafts of the text;

To John Condor Allie (PeaceLinks), Trish Appleton-Fox (Positive News), the Australia Tibet Council, Ahmet Bektas, Makeda Best (The Garden Project), Ellen Brogren (Peaceways), Isabel Buczinski, Olzod Bhum-Yalagch, Stephenie Cahalan, Alan Watson Featherstone, Friends of the Earth UK, Helen Gee, James Hallowell (PeaceLinks), Chris Harries, Barry Joseph (Global Kids), Vandy Kanyako (PeaceLinks), Margie Law, Claire Little (Brockwood Park School), Trevor Pemberton (Brockwood Park School), Justin Skinner (Arias Foundation), Bill Taylor (Brockwood Park School), Linda Wheeler (*Earth Garden* magazine), and Julie Whitman (Arias Foundation) – for their help with interviews, networking and research;

To Wirawat Theeraprasert, Margie Law, Noi Pornpen, Noel Rajesh and Suppamart Silarak for their generous contribution to interviews and translation;

To my parents Geoff and Julie Hawes, for their help and encouragement over many years;

To Kabir Jaithirtha, for his contribution to the Centre for Learning story;

To Jim Flynn and Pashwa Jhala, for many hours of deep inquiry;

To the creators of the My Hero website (www.myhero.com), which gave me many useful leads;

To Vera Gorge, for the inspiration;

To the people at Finch Publishing: in particular Rex Finch, for his faith in this project, and Sean Doyle, whose editing reinforced my belief that red ink is a writer's best friend. My thanks also to Nanette Backhouse, who created the book's inspired design.

I would like to say special thanks to Tamsin Whaley, whose six-page 'rave review' of one of my very early essays convinced me that *someone* out there was interested in what I was trying, however ineptly, to express; and to Helen Thomas, whose bold words challenged me to see the potential of the *Twelve Principles* project.

I am also particularly indebted to Bob Brown, who originally suggested the idea of drawing up a list of principles. Bob gave me invaluable help with the editing, and his encouragement helped me through times when I doubted my capacity to meet the challenges of this project. I'm honoured to have his foreword in this book.

I wish to acknowledge the enduring influence of J. Krishnamurti on my life and thinking, while emphasising that my own work does not attempt to represent his ideas.

Twelve Principles

This edition first published in 2003 in Australia and New Zealand by
Finch Publishing Pty Limited, PO Box 120, Lane Cove, NSW 1595, Australia.
ABN 49 057 285 248.

05 04 03   8 7 6 5 4 3 2 1

National Library of Australia Cataloguing-in-Publication entry
    Hawes, Martin, 1956- .
    Twelve principles: living with intergrity in the twenty-first century.

    ISBN 1 876451 48 3

    1. Progress. 2. Ecology. I. Title.
    303.44

Edited by Sean Doyle
Editorial assistance from Barbara Bessant
Text designed and typeset in Venetian 11.5pt and Optima 9pt on 15pt leading
    by saso content and design
Cover design by saso content and design
Printed in China by Everbest Printing Co. Limited

NOTES The 'Notes and resources' section contains additional information
about and source references for material quoted in the text. Each reference is
linked to the text by its relevant page number and an identifying line entry.

The paper stock used in this book is plantation-sourced.

Other Finch titles can be viewed at www.finch.com.au